Talking To the
Piano Player

Talking To the Piano Player

**Silent Film Stars, Writers
and Directors Remember**

by Stuart Oderman

BearManor Media
2005

Talking to the Piano Player:
Silent Film Stars, Writers and Directors Remember

© 2005 by Stuart Oderman

For information, address:
BearManor Media
P. O. Box 750
Boalsburg, PA 16827

bearmanormedia.com

Cover photo by Lena Tymczyna
Cover design by Lloyd W. Meek
Typesetting and layout by John Teehan

Published in the USA by BearManor Media

Library of Congress Cataloging-in-Publication Data

Oderman, Stuart, 1940-
Talking to the piano player : silent film stars, writers and
directors remember / by Stuart Oderman.
p. cm.
Includes bibliographical references and index.
ISBN 1-59393-013-5 (alk. paper)

1. Motion picture actors and actresses--United States--Interviews.
2. Motion picture producers and directors--United
States--Interviews. 3. Screenwriters--United States--Interviews. 4.
Silent films--United States. I. Title.

PN1998.2.O34 2004
791.43'092'273--dc22
2004023151

ISBN--1-59393-013-5

Acknowledgements

I am grateful to all of the interviewees for their willingness to share their recollections with such candor and honesty. I am also grateful to research archivist Ken Gordon.

To Janet Sovey and Tim Martin Crouse
with love and gratitude

"So here I am, being nostalgic,
and talking about the old days.
And I'm not talking to actors.
I'm talking to the piano player."

- Frank Capra, director
Conversation with author (1971)

Portions of this book have previously appeared in different forms:

Minta Durfee Arbuckle: *Films in Review*
Vol. XXXVI, No. 8/8 ©1985. Reproduced by permission of publisher
Editor/Publisher, Roy Frumkes
Website: www.filmsinreview.com

Leatrice Joy: *Films of the Golden Age*
No. 19, ©1999. Reproduced by permission of publisher
Editor, Bob King
Website: www.classicimages.com

Billie Rhodes: *Films in Review*
Vol. XXXIX, No. 12, ©1988. Reproduced by permission of publisher
Editor/Publisher, Roy Frumkes
Website: www.filmsinreview.com

Aileen Pringle: *Films in Review*
Vol. XLI, No. 3, ©1990. Reproduced by permission of publisher
Editor/Publisher, Roy Frumkes
Website: www.filmsinreview.com

Anne Pennington: *Films in Review*
Vol. XXXVII, No.5, ©1986. Reproduced by permission of publisher
Editor/Publisher: Roy Frumkes
Website: www.filmsinreview.com

Dorothy Davenport (Mrs. Wallace) Reid: *Classic Images*
January 2001, ©2001. Reproduced by permission of publisher
Editor, Bob King
Website: www.classicimages.com

Douglas Fairbanks, Jr.: *Films of the Golden Age*
No. 25, ©2001. Reproduced by permission of publisher Editor: Bob King
Website: www.classicimages.com

TABLE OF CONTENTS

Introduction

What do piano players, prostitutes, priests, bartenders, and hairdressers have in common?

They hear everything. Occupational frustrations, financial problems, political secrets, medical conditions, deaths, sexual infidelities: anything is liable to be the topic of the current moment. Only the settings and circumstances are different.

With the exception of the priests, whose answers are spiritual in nature, the responses of the others are generally very minimal, varying from an occasional nod to a few words of indifferent encouragement. When the customer is perhaps a little inebriated, the monotony and drudgery of his daily life are temporarily more bearable...until the next occasion of the next visit, and the process is repeated.

The listener has to be an expert in the art of listening. He is an available ear, which can easily be replaced with another available ear. Being a listener is a service occupation. The listener doesn't have specific hours.

I am what actor Eli Wallach calls, "the last of a dying breed," a working silent film pianist, whose travels from the Museum of Modern Art in New York, have taken him across the United States, Canada, and, on a few occasions, to the Athens Concert Hall in Greece. I have been creating music for faces for over forty-five years. Silent films, like old songs, evoke memories. Some are bitter, some are sweet.

Music has no language. Music crosses all cultural lines. You don't speak music. You listen to it. Music creates familiarity in the midst of unfamiliarity.

Silent film music is background. It accompanies the film. It is an undercurrent, like good air-conditioning. You don't know it is there, but when it isn't there, you sense something is missing.

Actors, away from their roles, are people, too. What they say on the stage or the screen are words that were written for their characters to say. The words are scripted and rehearsed.

The actors' responses, on these pages, are unrehearsed. They were said decades after the film in hotel lobbies, hotel kitchens, hotel bedrooms, and theatre wings. The silent faces we saw on the big screen in the dark are now talking and remembering...

Some actors had married once, and well. Some had never married. Some were involved in scandal. Some became recluses, choosing to live out their lives in furnished rooms on welfare checks.

They spoke about the good times, the bad times, people they liked and disliked, mistakes made in judgment...They wanted to set the record straight, *as they saw it.*

Even if only to a silent film pianist, who would continue to play for their work long after the final reels of their lives.

Everyone talks to a piano player. He has no choice, but to remain seated at his instrument.

If he listens, he'll hear almost everything...

■

Adela Rogers St. Johns

MALIBU: JULY 1972.

Adela Rogers St. Johns, the Hearst columnist and Mother Confessor of Hollywood, likes to talk.

To anyone who would listen.

If you want to ask a question, you have to wait until she takes a breath, and then you quickly seize the opportunity.

Her oceanfront house, like the other oceanfront houses, is a few steps from the beach. It is well away from the highway, and you cannot hear or see the steady stream of cars.

Her house is protected by electronically controlled gates which swing open once you have announced yourself, and have met with her approval. Nobody casually drops in for a visit, or a chat.

Adela, before the gates are opened, will tell you to pull your vehicle back a few feet before you move forward, and drive down a winding road to your parking space.

"I knew not to be right on the ocean," she will tell you, indicating the blue ocean and sandy beach just a few feet away from her spacious living room.

There are no autographed portraits on the walls of the old or new Hollywood. There are no framed book jackets of the books she has written, detailing her friendships with Mabel Normand or Jean Harlow, whose early tragic deaths were a great personal loss.

She is wearing an old bathrobe, and equally old bedroom slippers. It is three in the afternoon, and she makes no apologies for not being dressed. Somehow you, the visitor, should have been wearing a bathing suit. You could have gone for a swim, and she could have changed into something dressier.

But wait a minute! This is her house, and if she wants to receive you informally, take it as a compliment. Adela feels relaxed enough to see you without having to put on any Hollywood pretense. She isn't going anywhere. You came to see her.

"They all know me down here," she says. "The grocery store, the newspaper place, the post office. I've been here for years. I remember this area when it was brand new, and not too many people lived here.

"They didn't want actors. Actors were trouble. They attracted tourists, who were always trying to snap their pictures at times when they wanted privacy.

"Anna Q. Nilsson had a place down here, but she was accepted, because after she fell from that horse, her acting days were over.

"Thomas Ince was here, too.

"I can remember when the industry started a few miles away. This whole Los Angeles area was nothing but orange groves and a lot of sun. It gave the people from New York a few ideas. They were trying to get away from Thomas Edison, who had a low opinion of what was then called *flickers*.

Edison thought the *flickers* would have no future, except for illiterates and immigrants, who had only a few pennies to sit in some nickelodeon and watch trains pulling in and out of a station, or some people going for a day at the beach at Coney Island.

"Even with the tremendous success of *The Great Train Robbery* [1903], a one-reeler with a sustained narrative that really builds, he failed to see the potential of films.

"Men from the East like [Jesse] Lasky who was nothing but a trumpet player on a vaudeville circuit, saw what could be developed. He wasn't an educated man. He was a smart businessman, who had a lot of nerve.

"He saw that barn at the corner of Selma Avenue and Sunset Boulevard and he turned to his brother-in-law Samuel Goldwyn, and with Cecil B. DeMille, they pooled their resources, and they made *The Squaw Man*.

"It wasn't a one-reeler. It was a full-length film that starred Dustin Farnum.

"No unions. No politics like we have today. They just did it.

"That little barn became Paramount Pictures. But it was a little barn first.

"And they did their own distribution, too!

"I was working for Mr. Hearst at *The San Francisco Examiner* [1913] for $7 a week as a cub reporter, and the following year I was with *The Los Angeles Examiner*.

"Mack Sennett used to film right in Los Angeles on the streets in the Echo Park area with Charlie [Chaplin] and Mabel [Normand], and Roscoe Arbuckle, and the Keystone Kops. I don't know if he had to pay any high fees for permission, but he did let City Hall know what was going to happen.

"For the crowd scenes, Sennett used to employ local people as extras. They received a dollar a day, and they got a box-lunch. I'm sure some of those extras thought they were going to be discovered, but I don't think anything like that happened.

"You might have had a few amorous members of the crew looking for an hour's flirtation, but that was the way things were out here. Everybody knows, and nobody knows…unless somebody gets in trouble. Then you have a problem, and we had to cover it up the best way we could.

"A reporter is one kind of animal. A fan magazine writer is another, but the writing isn't much different. Both could help or hurt you.

"If you had good relations with either press, whatever problem you had could be glossed over in a monthly or weekly magazine. A newspaper could be quite deadly, if you had a major scandal.

"I worked for *Photoplay* magazine. Their circulation was star struck, impressionable young girls who saw the motion picture as an escape from their drab lives.

"If a new starlet seemed to have a certain quality that might register with the public, we had to create an earlier life for her. She could have been discovered at a restaurant. She might have been a rodeo rider. Maybe she was a librarian.

"Of course, a director just happened to *spot* her!

"Young girls all over the country believed it!

"And they came here by bus, or train, or with or without a chaperone, and a lot of dreams.

"It was faces, primarily faces in those days. Stage training was nice, and singing was nice, but we didn't have sound. Everything depended on how you *looked* on the screen.

"And some of the stories I used to hear were heartbreaking: they were small town beauty contest winners, or they got married to be able to get away from home, or they had a baby to support, or their man left them.

"A lot of these innocent hopefuls, male and female, could barely scrape together enough money to get here. And now they were here, and they didn't get that contract for thousands of dollars a week, and they had nothing to live on. How would they survive?

"At that moment these young hopefuls, male and female, became prey for anyone.

"A lot of those girls naturally went after Charlie [Chaplin] or he went after them. He had rooms at the beach. That's how it was done. He never pretended it was anything more. Innocence can only last a short time.

"We used code words and phrases: a weekend in Tiajuana, meant an abortion, or a Mexican vacation, or simply taking a few days' rest between assignments.

"It could mean anything: recovering from an alcoholic binge, or trying to slim down from overeating.

"The men always had it easier. Men didn't get pregnant. Hollywood, then and now, was always a man's town. If the lady was smart, she knew how to play the game, and she could survive.

"Lillian Gish was a survivor.

"Not so much Dorothy, her sister.

"Dorothy, in contrast to Lillian, was a girl who liked a good night on the town. She liked to party…without her mother.

"Lillian was quite the opposite. Lillian wore longer dresses. Sometimes she wore a bonnet, an old-fashioned-even-then bonnet like the ladies wore in covered wagons going to the Gold Rush of 1849.

"Mother Gish just doted over Lillian. Lillian was a few years older, and I think Mother Gish knew Lillian was the easier to control. Lillian was more ambitious, although Dorothy was the better actress.

"I do give Mrs. Gish a lot of credit. She saved her daughters from becoming prey to the wolves. And there were always wolves out here, and a little red riding hood.

"The acting profession was never, at least in those days, the type of profession that attracted well-educated girls from proper society.

"For girls on their very own, Hollywood was complete freedom. You had the studios, who were just starting, and you had the beaches.

"It was a very easy lifestyle to fall into, if you weren't that driven. If you didn't want to look for work, you went to the beach. There was constant sun, and there was always something going on. One person met another person. With a few more, you had a party.

"If you were a Lillian Gish, you avoided those parties. You concentrated on your work. There was no father in the Gish house. Only the mother. Everything depended on those girls.

"Dorothy always tried to get Lillian to go to the parties, but Lillian's socializing was concentrated on her director, D.W. Griffith. He was paying her salary.

"We used to have a name for the young girls who surrounded Griffith. We called them Griffith's Harem.

"But there was always a mystery about Lillian.

"We used to whisper, *Did she?* or *Didn't she?*

"Nobody could come up with an answer, and we tried to follow the two of them, but not let them see us.

"How could we really do that, and not be obvious?

"On some nights, it was the three of them: Lillian, Mr. Griffith, and her mother!

"The relationship of Lillian and Mr. Griffith will always be a mystery that will never be solved.

"Lillian loved her screen image. She seemed to live it off the screen, too.

"Jean Harlow hated, absolutely hated, her screen image. She wasn't this sex-crazy man-killer.

"Look at the men she married! I always thought Bill Powell would marry her, but he didn't.

"I once gathered the nerve to ask him why, and he said that one sex symbol, Carole Lombard, was more than enough.

"Carole Lombard was the most honest person I ever met. And gorgeous without trying to be, and down-to-earth.

"A lot of men out here are attracted to strong women, but in a marriage they want someone willing to put the husband first. No equal rights.

"I don't think Lillian Gish was much on equal rights. She wanted her own rights for herself, but she was able to maintain this *ethereal* quality.

"And that was what attracted the men. She wasn't easy, and some men like that quality.

"I guess that's all right. Up to a point.

"When Lillian walked into a room, men wanted to escort her to a table.

"When Jean walked into a room, men wanted to pinch her, or escort her *out* of the room...

"Mabel [Normand] was tragic: her life, her dealings with men, her death. One of the most tragic victimized people I ever met. She had spunk, she was a daredevil, and she could talk to any man on their level.

"She never concealed her face behind a fan, or played the coquette, or a damsel in distress the way Lillian would do.

"Mack was in love with her, and he wanted to marry her, but he was entirely too devoted and entirely too dominated by his mother, who never liked the motion picture business. No matter how much money he gave to his mother, she still saw the film industry as a dirty business. The people who worked in the film industry were little more than vagabonds.

"Mack's tragic flaw was that he was cheap. Maybe it came from being dominated by his mother. He was sitting on piles of money, and he did nothing with it.

"Even when he had Chaplin, Arbuckle, Mabel, and the Keystone Kops on the payroll and the studio was making a lot of money, Mack was cheap. He lived in rooms. Hotel rooms. The same kind of room's vaudevillians had when they were playing short stays in small towns, and they were cautious about their money, because they didn't know when the next booking was coming.

"He lost Chaplin, because he wouldn't give him a raise. He lost Arbuckle for the same reason.

"Mack never thought audiences could laugh longer than twenty minutes. Maybe that was why he stuck to one- and two-reelers, instead of features. Other studios were making full-length films. Not Mack.

"Perhaps his figuring ran to: the longer the film, the more it cost to make. And to a degree, he was right. But the full-length films made more money, if they were a hit.

"*Tillie's Punctured Romance*, which starred Mabel and Charlie, was made at Mabel's insistence. She threatened to leave him, and without her, he was lost. Charlie was popular, but Mabel was loved. And Mack knew that.

"That *Tillie's Punctured Romance* was a huge success came as a complete surprise to Sennett. He thought only a drama could hold the interest of an audience for more than twenty minutes.

"Sennett's next surprise was losing Chaplin. Chaplin wanted a reasonable raise, and Sennett wouldn't give it to him. Charlie, acting like a businessman, pointed out how much *Tillie's Punctured Romance* was grossing, and Sennett absolutely refused to listen.

"Sennett was cheap. Plain downright cheap. Tight. He hoarded his money like a *Silas Marner*.

"And he wasn't nicer to Mabel. There was no reason to treat her the way he did. He cheated on her, and she knew it. But until she actually caught him with Mae Busch she never had to actually face the situation: he was a scoundrel!

"Poor Mabel had a knack for picking the wrong men, and then being loyal to them, thinking that would win them over to her side.

"Poor darling Mabel! The most wonderful creature ever placed upon God's green earth. She wanted to marry Mack, and never did. He never married either, and they never got back together.

"And then poor Mabel entangled herself with Bill [William Desmond] Taylor!

"Taylor's death had all of the elements of a perfect whodunnit. His murder was a crime that will never be solved.

"His death was a crime nobody wanted to know much about. Some of us, who were on the inside, knew who killed him.

"The killer's identity had to be suppressed. If it made the papers, it would have killed the industry. It would have closed any chances of this industry continuing. Hollywood would have been broken right at the point when it was emerging from its infancy, and motion pictures were being recognized as a legitimate art form.

"Hollywood was never a town without scandal: drugs or sex related, but we knew how to keep those things quiet, and away from the public.

"A murder was something else.

"And a murder involving a young girl and an older man, who may or may not have been involved with her *mother* first…

"Mabel was one of the last people to have seen Bill Taylor alive.

"She never changed her story. I believed it then, and I believe it now. She had *nothing* to do with Taylor's murder!

"Mabel had gone to Taylor's bungalow, in the afternoon, to return a book of his she had borrowed.

"44-B South Alvarado, Taylor's bungalow, was in the Westlake district.

"Taylor had always lived alone, except for a butler, and a male secretary.

"Both Mabel and Taylor were book readers. He was a very literate man, which may have been the reason their relationship was probably more than a physical one.

"The male secretary may or may not have been Taylor's brother, but I'm not going to get into that. That's for the armchair detectives, and they won't solve the mystery either.

"I was right at that bungalow after I was telephoned by district attorney

Thomas Woolwine. He wanted me there *before* the police arrived.

"I had a few minutes to get to Taylor's bedroom by myself, remove any implicating evidence that would involve Mabel, and leave.

"I didn't have the chance to take everything. Just what might incriminate Mabel. I didn't think she had any reason to kill Taylor, but I didn't want the newspapers to turn this murder into a bigger circus.

"I rummaged through some of the drawers, and removed what I thought were Mabel's panties.

"I knew that Mary Miles Minter's nightgown and some of her love letters were there, but they weren't my concern.

"Only Mabel's welfare was on my mind. She wasn't the same since her planned wedding to Sennett was cancelled after he was caught with Mae Busch. Mabel found them together.

"Taylor was also a friend of Claire Windsor's, and she also had seen Taylor a few hours before the murder.

"The mother of Mary Miles Minter, Charlotte Shelby, was a very domineering woman who supervised every aspect of her daughter's life. She kept her a child, and she made her dress like a child. Mary was almost 18, but her mother tried to make her look like she was 12 or 13.

"It worked in some of her films, but over the short time she was on the screen, the little girl grew up. She matured. She developed breasts.

"Maybe Taylor liked this child-goddess, this Lolita-type. Maybe Mrs. Shelby was involved with Taylor, and her daughter was collateral…

"Maybe Taylor took a long, close look at Mary, and decided to switch affection…

"The story is simple to tell: one night someone shot William Desmond Taylor. The assassin was standing outside watching Taylor before he was shot.

"Neighbors who heard the shots said the killer was dressed like a man, but he *ran like a woman*!

"I knew why Woolwine called me: he and I knew who killed Bill Taylor. And he knew this case would kill the film industry. And he also knew that no jury would find Mrs. Shelby guilty. She was a mother who was avenging the moral wrong done to her daughter.

"So there was an investigation, but no killer was ever brought to justice.

"I know this sounds like one of those stories they used to publish in the penny-dreadfuls, but this was a different time. Hollywood was a western town with western values. It was a man's town, and if someone's young virginal daughter was taken advantage of, who would say any man was wrong to avenge this wrong-doing?

"And with the rumor circulating that the killer ran *like a woman...*

"What outraged mother would be found guilty?

"Of course, Mary's career virtually was over, and she stayed with her mother. Just the two of them: Mary and her mother. Together, until Mrs. Shelby died.

"Only God knows what they could have talked about all of those years.

"It was like the Lizzie Borden case. But Lizzie had a trial, and it was over.

"Mary never had the chance to see everything completed. Her life just came to a *sudden stop.*

"But the cars would continue to drive by. Some would stop, and hope to see if Mary peeked out occasionally from behind a curtain.

"Some say she had put on weight, and when *Whatever Happened to Baby Jane?* was released on the screen, that relationship could have been Mary and her mother.

"Sad."

Adela reached for her diet cola, as she sat down. Her face had become expressionless, like a windup toy that had completed its circuit.

She had said all that she had wanted to say. The presentation was over. I had heard something from film history from someone who had been present when it happened.

But I couldn't let this moment pass. Adela was looking at me, waiting for me to react, to say something, anything. A reaction. A question.

Hesitantly, I began.

"Mary Miles Minter told some people that she wanted to meet me."

"You mustn't," Adela answered. "Don't fall for it. Mary sometimes thinks that people are interested in her *career*. Her *career* is long over. And I don't think enough of her work survives that would attract an audience. Even if you were to play piano for it. What would she do in a question and answer session? The old Taylor case would come up. There's no way she could evade that. It has become part of the lore of old Hollywood.

"I can guarantee that if you met her, you would receive a lawyer's letter within the next few days. You would be accused of harassment.

"She tried to sue Rod Serling when he presented an episode on *The Twilight Zone* that had parallels to her situation. It was thrown out of court. Serling never accused anyone. The crime was never solved.

"But you knew who *inspired* the program...

"I was threatened with a lawsuit for briefly alluding to the Taylor case in my book, *The Honeycomb*.

"The charges were dropped, but it was a real pain-in-the-neck.

"Taylor's life and death will always be shrouded in mystery. That is the beauty of this industry. No matter who enters it, then or now, no one's life is publicized in the magazines as it really was.

"You can create your own past, and the studio can try to predict your future. The only problem is when you start to believe that what was created is the truth. The two eventually become intermingled. Nobody is hurt by it. People will always believe what they want to believe.

"Most of the scandals are forgotten...until somebody reviews old newspapers, and decides the scandal is ready for another airing.

"I never believed much about William Desmond Taylor, in his own time, or after. Too many loose ends.

"But that is what makes a good story. You keep talking about it. I'll leave the gates open."

■

Adela Rogers St. Johns and Stuart Oderman.

Marlene Dietrich

1970: THE MOROSCO THEATRE, NEW YORK

About Marlene Dietrich: there are legends and stories, and stories and stories, and stories and legends. It is hard to determine where one ends, and the other begins. Sometimes they intermingle, and there is a mixture of fact and fantasy. But it makes no difference. Miss Dietrich is a lady, and she is a survivor. She is a trouper who, like Greta Garbo, the star of G.W. Pabst's *The Joyless Street* (in which she was an extra in 1925), has created her own persona.

*Un*like Garbo, Marlene Dietrich is very approachable, if you have something to say beyond the usual compliments she has grown accustomed to hearing. Her presence on the street, or in a theatre lobby, will always cause a minor flurry of excitement, especially if she is alone. Observers will comment in whispers.

She is standing next to me. It is hard to deny that fabulous face, and those legs. She is not a stranger across a crowded room. We are waiting for the door to open.

I mumble something about Pabst's camera, and if Pabst were photographing this theatre lobby, instead of a breadline of destitute people in post-war Vienna, the camera would still favor her. The locations would be different, and a line is still a line, but some people are just more noticeable.

She smiles in acknowledgement, but it is a frozen smile, until I mention that I have played the piano for countless showings of *The Joyless Street*.

Now she turns and faces me directly.

She'll talk to you, I was told, *but only what she wants to talk about. Or she will politely walk away, as if nothing had been spoken.*

I start to mention a few of her German silents she made before *The Blue Angel.*

She lifts her hand slightly, as if signaling me to stop.

"I can't deny those silents, especially *The Joyless Street.* If people are watching them to see me, it's the wrong reason to look at them.

"*The Joyless Street* is a Garbo film. Early Garbo. Before she came to America. I had no contact with her. I was only an extra, and the star does not fraternize with the extras. Then or now.

"None of those films you were starting to mention ever did anything for me at the time, except pay the bills.

"We have to eat, and actors, like everybody else, take jobs to pay their bills.

"Silent films could be shown all over the world without making any adjustments, except in the titles. English, German, French: nobody ever thought of an actor's voice. A *voice* was for the stage.

"*The Joyless Street* paid my bills. It was about the drudgery of life after the war had ended. We could identify with that. Germans knew what had happened, and they could see the results everyday. The family, as we once knew it, was destroyed. Husbands left their wives, and children were put to work, even if only to earn a few pennies for a slice of bread. Meat, if you were able to get it, was at a premium. It was rationed.

"Of course, there were those who were often reduced to using sex as payment, but those were hard times. You just had to put your pride away. Not everybody resorted to sex. Some stole, some begged…

"The German cinema after the war, the European cinema after the war, stresses a realism that was almost non-existent in American films. A lot of American men lost their lives on the battlefield, but America won the war.

"I was appearing in a play [*Zewi Krawattan*] in Berlin [1929] in a very small role when Josef von Sternberg saw me, and asked me to report to his office. He had acquired a property, *The Blue Angel,* and Emil Jannings was already signed.

"Jannings was a great actor, and I was asked to play opposite him.

"During the shooting of the film, I could sense two camps forming: the von Sternberg camp, and the Jannings camp. I didn't like Jannings personally. I wasn't his type, and I wasn't going to get involved with him

Marlene Dietrich

on any level. I don't think he liked me. I don't think he liked anybody. I don't think he liked himself. I don't think he had any regard for himself. He had a very low sense of personal self-esteem.

"I knew if I wanted to keep any sort of career in films, or theatre, or cabaret, I would have to be an independent, and not align myself with anyone who was causing problems.

"The political scene had started to make its presence quite known: lootings of stores, street gangs of boys. Nobody took this as a warning of things to come.

"Erich Marie Remarque's *All Quiet on the Western Front* was now banned.

"I could have had anything I wanted, but I made up my mind to leave. Germany was beginning to succumb to madness.

"A lot of German actors and writers left: Fritz Lang, Erich Maria Remarque, Josef von Sternberg, Thomas Mann…

"Jannings made a highly successful film in California [*The Way of All Flesh*], for which he won an Oscar.

"Jannings chose *not* to stay in America. He chose to listen to Goebbels and return to Germany to make films for the Reich! He willingly returned.

"I could have stayed, and had anything I wanted. But I never agreed with their politics, and I knew what was happening wouldn't last forever. I wasn't going to be anyone's propaganda tool!

"Emil Jannings was born in Brooklyn, but he was raised in Germany. His mother was Jewish, but the Reich chose to overlook that. Where was Jannings' conscience? He used to say his accent was too thick, that American audiences wouldn't understand him, and his career wouldn't last very long in the sound era. He won an Oscar for a *sound* film, not a silent! Why did he go back to Germany?

"When he died [1950], there was a torchlight parade for him, and the newspapers said he was only a *nominal* Nazi.

"Their words, not mine. A *nominal* Nazi.

"Certainly he must have been aware of what was happening. There were a lot of Jews in the arts. And he must have known several.

"I did!

"I didn't return to Germany for years.

"When I finally went back and I saw Pabst, the first words he said to me were, 'Weren't those days horrible?'

"And I answered, 'I left. You chose to stay. If things were so *horrible*, as you say, why didn't you leave when some of the others did? You had every chance. Why did you stay?'

"Pabst didn't answer. He had no answer, like a lot of the others who chose to deny what was going to happen.

"Any fool with any knowledge of history knows that tyranny doesn't last forever. Free speech and freedom of thought may go underground for a while, but it never totally goes away. In the worst of times, there always was satire. As long as it was within *proper* boundaries.

"The younger generation is just daring to start asking questions about the past: *Where were you?* And *How could this have happened?*

"One day Germany will have to explain. Just answering, *You don't understand* is not enough.

"The older surviving generation will have to answer for their actions. Not to the Jews. Not to the world. But to themselves.

"And that will be very difficult.

She turns away momentarily.

"They're dimming the lights. I have to get my seat.

"Good luck!"

■

Marlene Dietrich.

Anita Garvin

1969: THE MASQUERS, HOLLYWOOD.
Forty-one years after Anita Garvin played opposite Stan Laurel and Oliver Hardy in *The Battle of the Century* (1927), and *Their Purple Moment* (1928), she is still the same statuesque, patrician beauty that made her a favorite with silent film audiences. At The Masquers, a social club for members of the entertainment industry, she is witty and more than willing to share her memories of the boys.

"I'll tell you something: It's good to see Laurel and Hardy on a big screen in front of an appreciative audience of pros: people in the business, who appreciate and love the work of fellow pros. Especially those two!

"Group laughter encourages more laughter. Some of us here can remember when these films were made. One- and two-reelers were always part of an evening's program. A lot of those shorts were better than the features they were supporting.

"Comedians like The Boys [Laurel and Hardy], and Buster [Keaton], and Charlie [Chaplin], made *audience* films. All of those men came to motion pictures from years of traveling stock companies, or vaudeville. They knew how to time their gags, and they were able to sense *screen*-time, which isn't the same as *stage*-time.

"Laurel and Hardy were the perfect screen team. Theirs was a balanced comedy, and they had perfect chemistry on camera. They could play off one another. They could improvise bits. But the controller was Stan, although the studio had a supervisor watching them.

"Wisely, they kept using the same supporting players: Edgar Kennedy, Jimmy Finlayson, Charlie Hall, Mae Busch. They had their own identities.

Anita Garvin with Laurel & Hardy.

The minute audiences saw them, they knew what to expect, even if they weren't able to identify them by name. They had recognizable faces. The closest thing to that kind of ensemble humor was the *Carry On* series, which came out of England in the 60's.

"I'm always asked if Stan and Ollie got along.

"They did, but I don't think it was a great friendship. They had a good, working, professional relationship, and there were never any temper tantrums or fighting for more time on-camera.

"They weren't in competition for the extra close-up. They weren't jealous of each other. Each had his own specialty. Ollie had the slow burn. Stan had the tears.

"Stan was the worker, the brains. He was Chaplin's understudy when they were touring as part of the Fred Karno Company. They played in the United States, but when they returned to England, Charlie decided to stay here. Stan went back, but Charlie wanted to try his luck in films.

"Remember: this was *before* Stan met Ollie. Ollie was born in America, and he was a vaudevillian, who played on showboats, and in stock companies. They happened, by sheer coincidence, to have appeared together in a short [*Lucky Dog*, 1917], but they didn't get together as the team we know until almost ten years later [*Forty-Five Minutes From Hollywood*, 1926].

"You can't watch that early sequence, and predict what they would become. Stan might have been thinner, and Ollie wasn't as heavy, but both of them were young, and the *team* chemistry wasn't there. They were just contract players.

"Everything is timing, and being there at the right time with what they want you to have. There's a two-reeler with Mabel Normand [*The Nickel Hopper*, 1919] where Ollie plays a dance band drummer, and Mabel's dance partner is Boris Karloff!

"Nobody knew about that film. It was discovered many years later. But what I am trying to say is that here were two *unbilled* major talents: Boris Karloff and Oliver Hardy, and the studio, while giving them employment, did not give them much recognition at that time.

"It's simply a case of being there, which I've said before. Mabel, with the help of Mack Sennett, was there at the right time. I was part of what you would call a stock company. I was busy, but I never had the opportunity to carry a picture. I think about it, when film collectors ask me why, but I can't complain, really. The camera was always nice to me, and I always got work.

"Visually the boys were perfect for the camera. A pair of opposites: thin and heavy. And the camera picked up on that. The moment you saw them, you had to laugh. And that was before they did anything. They also had great comic faces.

"Stan was always on the set before most of us. He would be constantly thinking of bits and gags to flesh out the story. He was aware of what the camera could do, and like most comedians with stage experience, a little afraid of it. What looked good on the stage was often different when it was put on film. The camera blew things up. There are no balconies as far as a camera is concerned. No matter where you sit, it's the same picture.

"There was a lot of laughter behind the camera when we were shooting, but that was typical of moviemaking in those days. Sometimes another film was being shot a few feet away, and you had all you could do to maintain your concentration.

"Some directors would talk you through your performance, telling you what to do, as you were doing it. [D.W.] Griffith often did that. He'd count out loud, because he wanted a scene to be timed a certain way. With the boys, they counted in their head. They had natural timing. Timing can't be taught. You either have it, or you don't.

"I'll tell you a little gossip about Stan. He was a notorious, big-time, ladies' man. A lot of those comedians were. Charlie, especially. Stan was always involved with some girl. A lot of girls came to Hollywood, hoping to be movie stars. Some did get work. Most didn't, and they stayed around, looking for a man to marry them.

"Stan used to say Ollie's hobby was golf, and his hobby was marriage. He married eight of his hobbies, and there was almost a ninth!

"Ollie had two wives. His first wife died, and he remarried. Both were lovely ladies, and very supportive.

"Ollie wasn't an early riser, unless he wanted to be on the golf course. He didn't report to the set early. He left everything to Stan. Stan handled all of the set-ups. Then Ollie would come in a few hours before the actual shooting time, and he'd learn his blocking. Nothing was ad-libbed during the actual shooting, because it was all timed. We had to shoot a reel a week.

"Stan would see those golf clubs in Ollie's dressing room, and he would get very upset. Here he was: up all night, and Ollie would come in, listen to what Stan wanted him to do, and then do it in a minimum amount of takes. Then he would go back to his dressing room, change his clothes, pick up his golf clubs, and, if there was enough time, head back to the golf course.

"Stan would look at the rushes, but Ollie rarely did, unless he had to. He left everything up to Stan.

"Stan was the artist. Ollie was the businessman. Maybe that was why they lasted. There were no egos at stake. Laurel and Hardy were two professionals, who showed up for work. They did their jobs, and went home. No fuss. No fights.

"You can't have it any other way."

■

Frank Capra

1971: WOR-TV, CHANNEL 9, NEW YORK.

Nostalgia never dates. As we move ahead, it takes us back to the recent, and sometimes distant past. For some inexplicable reason, the olden days of decades ago are always better. Especially the movies, the plays, the books, and the music. The movies had real stars, the plays were more sophisticated, the novels were better written, and the music was hummable.

The Joe Franklin Show, long a staple on New York late night television, has combined the newest of the rising stars, providing the first exposure to then-newcomers Barbra Streisand, Woody Allen, Bill Cosby, as well as veteran performers like Rudy Vallee, Allan Jones, and Buddy Rogers. Joe's audience reflects a cross-section of the city.

On tonight's show, the guests include Artie Shaw, the bandleader, and film director Frank Capra. Shaw is on hand to announce another re-issue of a compilation of *Artie Shaw's Greatest Hits,* which includes the inevitable "Begin the Beguine," "Dancing in the Dark," "Frenesi," and "Summit Ridge Drive."

Frank Capra will be talking about the release of his autobiography, *The Name Above the Title.*

Shaw and Capra, although they are certainly aware of each other's accomplishments, have never met.

In the Green Room, prior to the taping of the program, both men exchange pleasantries for a few minutes until Shaw cynically says, "There's no escape. I liked this music when I recorded it originally, but now it haunts me. It's time to move on. Nobody wants to drive a '38 Chevy. How old is the generation that will buy these reissues?"

Capra smiles, and shrugs his shoulders. His career dates from the silent era, and Joe Franklin, as a surprise to Capra, will be showing clips from a Capra-directed feature *Tramp, Tramp, Tramp*, which stars Harry Langdon and a young Joan Crawford, who is at the start of a career that will endure as long as Capra's.

Capra smiles. He thought he would be talking about *It Happened One Night* and *It's a Wonderful Life*.

In the studio I am seated at the piano. A monitor is next to me.

"I'll tell you some stories after the taping," Capra says.

"When I was hired to work in the film business," Capra starts, "I was a gag writer for Hal Roach. I had to think of funny situations for the *Our Gang* comedies. They were fun, and Hal Roach was a nice man to work for.

"When I went to work at [Mack] Sennett's in 1924, I saw that his place wasn't the *Fun Factory* on which the studio had established their reputation. Don't get me wrong. The studio was still operating, but three of the good people that put Keystone on the map had left. [Charles] Chaplin had a salary dispute, [Roscoe "Fatty"] Arbuckle was finished, because of the San Francisco hotel scandal, and Mabel [Normand] had personal problems, which made her unreliable.

"Sennett was a simple man with a simple sense of humor. He never thought he was above his audiences. If a gag made him laugh, he thought everyone would laugh.

"If a comedian could quickly establish his identity within a few seconds of his initial screen appearance, the audience would do the rest.

"I quickly learned from Sennett that the secret of silent film comedy is props.

"Props are the trademarks that give a comedian a distinct personality of his own. A comedian in silent films had no voice. He only had his body, and his face.

"Audiences saw a derby and a cane, they knew it was Charlie Chaplin. Oliver Hardy also had a derby, but he didn't have a cane. Arbuckle had a derby, but he also had Luke, the dog. All of the Keystone Kops wore a derby. The British called them bowlers.

"Sennett thought a mustache in itself was funny. Just look at Chaplin. Then look at Mack Swain, and Charlie Chase, and Raymond Griffith. All had mustaches, which became part of their personnas.

"Sennett liked to poke fun at figures of authority, particularly police-

Frank Capra.

men. He made these officers of the law disorganized, and as soon as audiences saw them, they started to laugh hysterically. Sennett knew he struck a chord.

"D.W. Griffith, for whom Sennett worked, disagreed violently. To Griffith, the police were protectors of law and order. Not to Mack. To him nothing was sacred. You could poke fun at any institution. Especially law and order.

"For reasons Sennett couldn't explain, he gave Harry Langdon a contract.

"A few of us were called in, and we watched a reel of Langdon's vaudeville act, which Mack had filmed.

"Langdon was almost 40 years old. He had a puffy baby's face that looked like it was covered with white powder blended into his skin. He wore a hat, naturally, and his jacket was one or two sizes too small. It was buttoned incorrectly. The buttons weren't going into the right holes, which gave the jacket a lopsided look.

"His prop, against which he played, was a car, a very old, beaten-up car. The car would shake, and he would shake his finger at the car, as if to say, 'Naughty, naughty.' And then he'd look at the camera with those big eyes…

"We were told to develop this new arrival. Sennett liked him: this 40-year-old baby-faced man, who thought he was Charlie Chaplin!

"Langdon didn't have Chaplin's muscular body that some women found attractive. If ladies ever went for Langdon, we thought they would try to *mother* him. Not anything else.

"'What do you think?' Sennett asked, after the lights were turned on.

"Nobody said a word. We all sat in total silence. Had Sennett gone crazy? Usually there was laughter, or discussion. But this time, nothing was said. Was Sennett trying to play a trick on us? Was this an April Fool's joke?

"'Don't you like him?' Sennett asked again.

"And again there was no response. It was obvious we didn't like him. And nobody had seen Langdon in the flesh yet!

"'Well, I signed him,' Sennett said, and he was angry. 'You come up with something that can put him across!'

"We ran that vaudeville filmed act again, and again.

"Langdon worked *slow*, very slow. It was his innocence, his continuing innocence in the face of these situations that we would have to utilize.

"Langdon was simple innocence, and trust. He'd be baffled by butterflies. His character would trust everybody, and he would believe in everything…

"I don't think Langdon ever understood his screen character from the moment he started with two-reelers, into the four features I directed [*The Strong Man* and *Tramp, Tramp, Tramp*, 1926; *His First Flame* and *Long Pants*, 1927].

"The films were reasonably successful. A young Joan Crawford was his leading lady in *Tramp, Tramp, Tramp*. She was beautiful, and ambitious, and she worked hard not to laugh. There were some sequences where she had to face away from the camera, because she kept breaking up, and we couldn't afford to waste so much time and feet of film.

"Langdon's stardom came almost immediately, and he really didn't know how to handle his sudden celebrity. A year before he stepped in front of a camera, he was a barely surviving vaudevillian performing in tank towns.

"He began to think that his success was due to himself, and not the studio. He had quickly forgotten how hard we worked to create a screen persona. He constantly asked for more *bathos*, thinking that was Chaplin's secret.

"We tried to make him keep the character that had worked for him, but he wouldn't listen any longer.

"So Langdon left Sennett, and formed his own company: Harry Langdon Productions.

"He wanted no part of me. He didn't want to have anything to do with me. He didn't want me to work for him. I was holding him back from becoming another Chaplin!

"Langdon wanted to be everything Chaplin was: an actor, a director, a writer. He wanted more Chaplin-like sentimentality in his films, and I was preventing it. He didn't realize that Chaplin's sentimentality came out of the character he was playing.

"Langdon was just pathetic looking. He thought just keeping the camera on his face was enough.

"It wasn't. And you could see that in the films where he was in complete control. He got everything he wanted, because he had the money to pay for it.

"Harold Lloyd knew how to surround himself with a creative team. Harry Langdon only wanted to have people who would agree with whatever he wanted to do.

"I wasn't going to lick his boots, even if it meant holding a job. My name was on the screen, too, and I wasn't going to be associated with someone who was going to direct me how to direct him!

"So I went to Columbia, a studio we called, 'The Germ of the Ocean.'

"In those days, Columbia was a Poverty Row operation. It was little more than a few shacks.

"Harry Cohn ran Columbia, and I knew his bark was worse than his bite. What mattered most to him was how much money your film made, and how much did it cost, and did you keep the cost down? Very basic reasoning that all of those studio chiefs had. Harry was more blatant about it.

"But Harry Cohn survived, when the others didn't. And there had to be a reason for it.

"I had my reason for going to work for him: I was out of work. Harry Cohn knew my work. He wanted me, and I needed him. Very simple. We met, we talked, and I was hired.

"Years later someone told me the only pictures Harry Cohn would watch over and over again starred The Three Stooges. They made shorts, and they were low budget.

"The Three Stooges had his kind of humor: common.

"Shorts rounded out the programs, and there were a lot of common people who liked the Stooges. And those shorts were cheap to make.

"My early features for Harry Cohn were low budget programmers. They were done quickly, inexpensively, and they were entertaining.

"*That Certain Thing*, which starred Viola Dana, took about six weeks to shoot, and we saved money.

"I'll tell you how: the story was about a restaurateur's son who wants to be an active part of his father's business. He wants to advance, but he's fallen in love with a girl from the wrong side of the tracks.

"Naturally, the father disowns him.

"We have a good contrast: rich boy, poor girl. Audiences love that sort of thing.

"The boy and girl are in love, and they have to survive. They have to earn a living. What can they do?

"Easy! Box-lunches! Box-lunches can be sold to the neighborhood folks. Everybody loves this girl, and they are willing to help them out.

"The box-lunches are a hit, and they so successful that the wealthy father is being forced out of business.

"Realizing what is going to happen, the father takes his son back.

"The son also makes his father accept the girl he loves. The restaurant business and the box-lunch business come together, and the son is made the president of this new enlarged restaurant!

"He asks the girl to marry him. She says yes. The End.

"We also made *flapper* pictures. A flapper was the name given to a young lady of that time, who was unconventional. That meant she went to parties at unusual hours in unusual places, and she stayed out late. And she possibly might have a drink or two, just to keep her boyfriend interested in her.

"She may sometimes drink too much, and she might dance a wild Charleston on the top of a table, but underneath that wild exterior is a really nice girl, who is looking for a nice boy.

"The secret, when you made those films, was to keep your audiences guessing. At what point will the heroine realize that time is passing her by? At what point will the hero realize that the true love he is searching for is right under his nose?

"We all need someone to love, to give us a home and security, to cook for us, and provide a living to support a family. All of these things were part of the values those audiences brought with them to the movie theatres.

"We turned out the kind of product they wanted.

"The actors at Columbia, and the directors, and the writers, too, weren't working for MGM salaries, and a lot of people thought Columbia was a fly-by-night operation.

"Somehow we survived, and when the sound era came, we were still in business. We didn't go under, but we weren't turning out constantly guaranteed successes all the time. Despite the schedule, we weren't an assembly line, as some people like to think.

"We tried to tailor each film to the actor we were able to get. A lot of our actors were sent to us from major studios as punishment. They were still under contract, but they wouldn't toe the line.

"[Clark] Gable was one, and Louis B. Mayer at MGM sent him over to us. We took him, because we had to, and we used him in *It Happened One Night*, which was a huge hit. We were able to get Claudette Colbert because she was taking a four-week vacation.

"Working at Columbia may have been considered a step down in the industry, but it wasn't an artistic one. Many of our films: *Lost Horizon, Mr. Deeds Goes to Town, Mr. Smith Goes to Washington* are classics that are still shown in revival houses, university campuses, film schools, and on late night television. Those films will always have an audience.

"It really galls me to hear the current studio executives talk about how much money *The Godfather* brought in. *The Godfather* had a five-dollar admission ticket. Five dollars!

"When films like *Lost Horizon* and *It Happened One Night* were made in the thirties, the ticket price in the major cities was fifty cents! For every person who paid five dollars to see *The Godfather*, ten people, *ten* people could have seen one of my pictures!

"Who had the *larger* audience?

"It was because of attitudes like the one I mentioned that drove me out of the business of picture-making!

"There always existed the credo that you were only as good as your last picture, but when I made my films I mentioned, I had total creative control. But I had put years in before that happened.

"When I made *A Pocketful of Miracles*, which turned out to be my last picture, although I didn't know it at the time, I had no control at all. No control over the casting. I had to take Glenn Ford's girlfriend at the time. And I wouldn't kowtow to Glenn Ford anymore than I would kowtow to Harry Langdon.

"But Harry Langdon was the old days, and after thirty-five years, I could see the attitude of trying to tell the director how to direct hasn't changed. Glenn Ford wasn't like Langdon, and he started at Columbia, too!

"I had to deal with Glenn Ford, and too many people with too many ideas.

"*A Pocketful of Miracles* wasn't an easy film to make, and it should have been.

"The reviews weren't the kindest.

"Maybe the audiences had changed. Maybe sentimentality had been replaced with this anti-everything attitude that said nothing was worth living for. A picture with heart was no longer in fashion.

"Maybe this was a warning to get out.

"So I got out.

"I had a good run. Nothing to be ashamed about.

"So here I am, being nostalgic, and talking about the old days to the piano player in a local movie house. And I'm not talking to actors. I'm talking to the piano player."

■

Stuart Oderman and Frank Capra.

Anita Loos

1970: THE POETRY CENTER OF NEW YORK AT THE 92ND STREET Y.

In existence for over half a century, the 92nd Street Y has played host to the world's most honored writers, including T.S. Eliot, Arthur Miller, William Styron, Arthur Koestler, and Truman Capote.

Capote, holding a ball point pen in one hand, and a sheaf of full-sized legal pads in the other, read to an invited audience for two nonstop hours from the manuscript of *In Cold Blood*, then a work-in-progress, making corrections as he judged the audience reaction.

The lobby is again crowded, and I am standing in the corner with novelist Glenway (*The Grandmothers, The Pilgrim Hawk*) Wescott, Janet Planner, a Paris correspondent for *The New Yorker*, who writes under the name Genet, and screenwriter-novelist Anita Loos, best known for *Gentlemen Prefer Blondes*, which was also a hit Broadway play [1926], a silent film [1928], a Broadway musical [1949], and a Marilyn Monroe movie musical [1953].

"What's sad about the silent film," Anita Loos says, "is that it is lost forever. Like so many silents, it was allowed to disintegrate due to neglect, and I never got a print of my own. Mary [Pickford] always had copies of her own films. Gloria Swanson had personal prints, but I never thought about it. I thought those films would always be there for us.

"Once the film was completed, and it had its premiere, I forgot about it. The job was finished, and I went on to the next assignment. I think a lot of us did. To us, these films were Jobs. Some were good, some weren't. We didn't get royalties as writers on a film. Only books gave us royalties.

"When sound came in, nobody ever thought these films would be seen again. There were no such things as revival houses to keep these films alive, even to a limited audience. The word *film-buff* wasn't even in our vocabulary.

"The process of turning from silents to sound took about two years. Some films, if they could be completed as silents, were. Others were called "part-talkie." Usually the second half was the sound portion, for obvious reasons.

"A lot of theatres were very reluctant to spend all of that money converting from silents to sound. Nobody knew how long sound would last. Griffith, who came out of the theatre, where he could barely earn a living, and didn't know where the next job was coming from, or if there would be a next job, suddenly became one of the theatre's staunchest defenders, saying that spoken words belonged on the stage, not a screen, where the actors would have to gather around a flower pot to speak their lines, because microphones weren't very reliable, and the sound levels distorted their actual voices.

"When Griffith made silents, nobody ever thought of sound. You didn't need sound, because you had titles to tell the story. And the titles could be written in any language. You never had to worry about people in Europe, who didn't speak or understand English.

"When you went to nickelodeons in the early days of the *flickers*, you hardly had any titles. The audiences were immigrants who couldn't read quickly or well.

"We used the *snore level* as a way of judging those films. If you heard too many people snoring, you were in trouble. It meant that you weren't holding their interest. What was worse was that somebody had to wake those sleepers up and get them out, so the next audience would be able to come in.

"Eventually, as Americans grew up, so did motion pictures. The camera photographed America for everyone to see. It brought people together with a story told with simple gestures and body movements.

"But it was a stationary camera. Only in one position. You saw a whole body on the stage, and you saw a whole body on the screen, until Griffith realized that the camera eye didn't work like the human eye. You stood *next* to people in real life, and when you looked at them, you didn't see their feet, did you? You only saw their faces. You didn't ask yourself, 'Where are their legs?'

"Griffith realized that motion picture cameras could emphasize what was most important to that scene. The motion picture was a story for the screen, told not by words, but by images. It was another kind of narrative, and Griffith knew he would need a steady supply of all kinds of stories to put on that screen, if he wanted to make a living. He had to provide entertainment for paying customers every week.

"I grew up in a world of words and stories. My father was a California newspaper man, and we lived between San Francisco and Los Angeles, and San Diego and Los Angeles. I heard him tell stories of what he had to cover all the time.

"I started writing my own stories and poems when I was about seven or eight. I knew how to read, and the more I read, the more I wanted to keep reading.

"It was the same way with writing. The more words I got down on those yellow second-sheets, the more I wanted to keep writing.

"I wanted to be like my father. I wanted to know about everything, and write about everything. At the age of seven or eight, no subject is unapproachable.

"My mother was a plain, unsophisticated housewife, who cooked and cleaned. Her daily life was constant drudgery, and maybe seeing that constant drudgery and how she was trapped by it, and too powerless or afraid to do anything about it, or fearful what the neighbors would say, affected me.

"Children, who are at home a lot in their early years, see a lot of things, are witness to a lot of things they can't verbalize.

"I just knew I didn't want my life to ever be like my mother's.

"Girls were just girls until they entered their teen years. And then their lives centered on finding a man, the right man, who could take care of you. And in return, you can cook and clean for them the way your mother cooked and cleaned for your father. And have a few children, too.

"I had some poems and little stories in my father's newspaper. I was very proud of what I had accomplished. I was a writer, and I saw my words in print, and I knew people would read them, people I didn't know.

"I probably had little dolls the way other little girls did, but I liked being printed in a newspaper better. I didn't have a typical childhood, but I wasn't deprived of anything. Certainly my father loved me, and that was important.

"I think my father sent one of my stories, "The New York Hat," to

D.W. Griffith at Biograph in New York. Or maybe he told me to send it out.

"Biograph was on 11 East 14th Street, and one of us heard that Griffith was in the market for stories.

"This was in 1912.

"I signed my name, 'A. Loos.' I was afraid that Griffith wouldn't read anything written by a girl, and I may have been thinking of Sir Arthur Conan Doyle, the Sherlock Holmes writer, who signed his name, 'A. Conan Doyle.'

"You can imagine my surprise when a letter came with a check for $25, made out to 'A. Loos!'

"My father was very proud of me. That was a lot of money.

"So I sat down, and I wrote more stories that I sent to Mr. Griffith. Maybe I sent three stories.

"I don't think they were as long as "The New York Hat," but they were comic, and I only received $15 for each story.

"But that was fine. A writer has to write, and then sell the product. I could crank out those stories like laundry.

"I just knew that someone wanted my words, and was willing to pay for them, and turn them into movies. I was a writer like my father, and I wanted to write for the movies!

"When you make a decision like that, especially when you're barely into your teens, it's an important moment. You are breaking away from your family, and you are thinking about yourself and your future. You are stepping out on your own, and it is a very selfish thing to do: to try to take control of your life, and take responsibility for your actions. If you fail, you can't blame anybody but yourself.

"Girls or young ladies of that era weren't allowed to think that way. It wasn't ladylike, we were told, and men wouldn't want someone who was outspoken, and didn't know her place. A woman's place was in the home, doing the cooking and cleaning, and raising the children.

"Men were the providers. My brother had more formal education than I had. He had a university education, and he went into medicine. He started a plan of medical coverage we call Blue Cross.

"I wanted to be a writer for the films. My mother thought films were trash, and people in them were trash, and anyone who associated with them...

"Of course, this was always said *after* the performance. I don't think she ever allowed herself to actually like what she was seeing. She preferred to stay at home. Or maybe she was afraid to leave the house without my father.

"This first New York check only fired up my ambition. It increased my desire to do what I wanted to do. And I had my father on my side.

"I had it all planned, I'd write them, sell them, and get a check within two or three weeks. Just like that: very simple.

"Nowadays it isn't so simple. Everything is agented, and all that goes with it.

"But in those days, the motion picture business was in its infancy. Lines of hopefuls were around the block. Everyone was waiting to be discovered. And these were just the people off the street. You also had a lot of stage people, who needed quick money until the stock company job came.

"I was doing some acting with a stock company on the San Diego area when I was sending out stories. My mother didn't appear to be pleased with that either.

"There was no need to worry about my acting talent. I wasn't any good, but I was good enough to get hired and make a few dollars, while I was trying to decide what to do with my life.

"I knew I had to break away from my family, and I eloped with a musician. It wasn't the smartest thing to do, but it was a decision I made on my own.

"It didn't last, and I had to come home...

"When Griffith sent for me, I thought it would be wise for me to have a chaperone for the sake of propriety. Griffith was in Los Angeles, and he still thought *A. Loos* was a man!

"When I showed up with my mother, he asked us, 'Where is A. Loos?'

"My mother said, There isn't any A. Loos. I was *Anita* Loos!

"He looked down at me, shrugged his shoulders, and didn't say anything else.

"Mary Pickford and Lionel Barrymore had the leads in *The New York Hat*. They were hired at $5 a day when they first started. All of the actors received $5 a day, and no billing. It was a way of keeping some control, since everyone was equal.

But Mary and her mother were quite aware of all of the nickels and dimes that were constantly coming in from all over the country. Mary pressured Griffith, and she got a raise.

"Mr. Griffith should have known, more than anybody else, how important salaries were to an actor. Before he became a director, he was an actor. He was a *failed* actor, and then he became a *failed* playwright.

"He went into films because there was nothing else he could try, and films were new. That he found his true voice was a total surprise to him, because I don't think he intended to stay in films.

"I think he believed films were a temporary job. The actors he hired were theatre actors who felt the same way. The *flickers* might damage your theatre career, if it became known you were doing too many of them.

"But the money was better, and steadier. You just had to put your artistic pride aside…and take the work!

"Don't forget that Lillian [Gish] was in *The New York Hat*. She won't talk about it, because she likes to date her career from *An Unseen Enemy*, which came out around the same time, and Dorothy [Gish], was also in it.

"In *The New York Hat*, and don't tell Lillian what I'm saying, you can clearly spot her in the crowd that has gathered outside the church after the service. You have to look closely. Lillian is wearing a plain coat, which was probably her own.

"Mr. Griffith wasn't going for realism by having Lillian wear her own coat. He was just cutting corners, and trying to save money.

"Mrs. Gish, Lillian's mother, occasionally helped out in the wardrobe department as a seamstress. Sometimes she was in the crowd scenes, and sometimes she was there to act as *Lillian's* chaperone!

"You'll notice I said Lillian, and not Dorothy. Dorothy wanted no part of being chaperoned. She was quite independent her whole life. Lillian did everything her mother wanted *her* whole life.

"When Mrs. Gish had her stroke years later, Lillian was working in Rome, and Dorothy was in New York taking care of everything: doctors, nurses.

"But Mrs. Gish wanted *Lillian* to take cafe of her.

"So Lillian came home from Rome, and had to take over Dorothy's chores.

"Mrs. Gish was put in a wheelchair, and covered with a *sable* lap robe Lillian got especially for her. And then Lillian, and Lillian *only*, pushed Mama in that wheelchair with the sable lap robe along Fifth Avenue on the sunny days for everyone to see.

"Lillian, her mother used to say, pushes the wheelchair the way I like it.

"Whatever Mrs. Gish wanted, Mrs. Gish got!

"The motion picture industry, in those early days, was fueled by driven mothers. Most of them were uneducated, unskilled housewives whose husband's income was inadequate, or they were without husbands, and they had to take charge themselves.

"These movie mothers, or stage mothers, were the breadwinners, but it was the children who were doing the actual providing. Besides Mrs. Gish, and Mrs. Smith, who was the mother of Mary and Jack Pickford, there was Richard Barthelmess' mother. Mrs. Gish didn't want her Lillian to fall in love with Richard, and she hoped Dorothy wouldn't fall in love with Robert Harron.

"If you want to study mothers-in-contrast, you have to watch Mrs. Gish and Peg Talmadge. She had three daughters: Constance, Norma, and Natalie.

"Mrs. Talmadge wanted to be called 'Mother' Talmadge.

"'Mother' Talmadge was the direct opposite of Mrs. Gish.

"Mrs. Gish wanted her daughters to avoid men. 'Mother' Talmadge wanted her daughters to *look* for men. But only the right kind of man: a man with money!

"And those Talmadge girls did! They all married men with money!

"Norma married movie mogul Joe Schenck, and later Broadway actor Georgie Jessel, who had the leading role in the play, *The Jazz Singer*, which became the first Hollywood sound film. Jessel made a very silly mistake: he thought sound was a novelty, and wouldn't last. So he turned down the chance of being in the film. Had he made the film, instead of Al Jolson, be would have made even more money.

"Natalie Talmadge married Buster Keaton, Constance Talmadge, on a dare from Dorothy Gish, married Greek stockbroker John Pialoglou.

"Connie's marriage was an elopement, which was considered scandalous, because it meant you were running away from a disapproving family.

"Dorothy Gish also eloped.

"I think both girls wanted to break away from their mothers, who were running their lives.

"Jim Rennie, Dorothy's husband, was a successful Broadway actor, and there was some money there.

"Mrs. Gish and 'Mother' Talmadge were very domineering, and I think Dorothy and Connie wanted to have control over their own lives. To be pampered by a man is a very desirable thing.

"Of course, it's always that way in the beginning. Neither Dorothy nor any of the Talmadge girls really wanted careers.

"I think Lillian wanted a career. Maybe playing somebody else was the only time and way she could get away from her life she had off-stage. Mrs. Gish never allowed Lillian to have any real boyfriends, whose love might take Lillian away from her.

"Eventually Jim Rennie left, and the husbands of the Talmadge girls left, and all of the girls realized their mothers were *right*. This is what happened when you stopped listening to your mother.

"The man who got the worst of it was poor Buster. When his drinking became unbearable, and when his money started to dwindle, Natalie took their two sons, and divorced him. She also *changed* the *last* names of the boys to hers, and he never saw them again.

"'Mother' Talmadge made sure that all of her daughters had trust funds in their own names. And their husbands couldn't get anywhere near those trust funds.

"Dorothy Gish and the Talmadge girls: they all had terrible marriages.

"So they went back to their careers.

"Things were okay for a short time, until something called *sound* came in. And when it was no longer a novelty, and people like Georgie Jessel realized they had made a disastrous mistake in judgment and this *novelty* couldn't be ignored, you could almost predict what was going to happen.

Some actors, who looked good, couldn't talk. And some, who looked good, didn't have the voice that went along with their face.

"You saw careers being destroyed almost overnight.

"A lot of actors began secretly to go to voice coaches.

"Some took singing lessons.

"Anything to keep their career going.

"It worked for some, but not for many.

"Dorothy and Lillian made a few early sound films, but they weren't successful. Lillian always blamed poor sound as the primary reason. Luckily they were able to return to the stage, where they had originally performed when they were children.

"For the Talmadge girls it was just about over. Constance and Natalie never made the transition. They avoided having to try. Norma made a few sound films, but she didn't have enough of a voice without sounding ridiculous.

"Not one of the Talmadge girls was upset. 'Mother' Talmadge, with the help of trust funds and some alimony from their later marriages, knew how to protect her daughters.

"They never really wanted to have a career in any motion picture, silent or sound.

"Although none of the Talmadges would even voice an opinion regarding sound, I think they were afraid of it, like so many actors.

"Charlie Chaplin and Greta Garbo had great fears regarding sound.

"When Garbo finally made her sound debut in *Anna Christie*, the studio's publicity department issued what became a world-famous headline: *Garbo Talks!*

"John Gilbert? Well, you know what happened to him.

"It was the end of an era. Movies had learned to talk. The sounds you heard outside the theatre were almost identical to the sounds you heard inside the theatre. Sound was here to stay, and movies had lost their innocence.

"Hooray for Hollywood!"

■

Allan Dwan

1980: LOS ANGELES: THE LOS ANGELES HILTON HOTEL

At a few minutes after nine in the morning, there are only four types of people on Hollywood Boulevard: the hopefuls, the tourists, and the prostitutes and hustlers. All are easily identifiable. The hopefuls are waiting to be discovered like Lana Turner at Schwab's drugstore, the tourists photograph anyone who looks the least acceptable, the hustlers are trying to find an area where the sun will shine directly on them, making them seem more desirable, and the prostitues make adjustments with age.

Legends are born on Hollywood Boulevard. Someone was discovered just walking, and a studio mogul saw them, stopped his chauffeured limousine to offer an immediate contract.

Was it Cary Grant?

Was it Rudolph Valentino?

Occasionally a story of Mae Murray eating lunch near the window of the Hollywood Roosevelt in the early sixties is heard. Mae was the Widow to John Gilbert's Prince Danilo in the celebrated MGM 1925 production of the famous Lehar operetta. That she sometimes has memory lapses, and dines and greets some of the Roosevelt patrons in her *Merry Widow* costumes 40 years later only added to the charm of the old Hollywood. Nobody laughed, and Mae was ever so gracious in acknowledging those who applauded her in the hotel, or on the sidewalk.

The studio might be trying to reach me, she would say, *and I have to be in an area where I am easily seen. The management is always so nice to me, but they have to make sure my table is available. Sometimes it isn't.*

The studio is aware of these things. I never had these problems in the old days. The only problem is there aren't many people left from the old days…

Two are left: director Allan Dwan, and cameraman Arthur Miller whose respective careers began with a 1909 apprenticeship under D.W. Griffith, and working for George Fitzmaurice in 1911.

They see each other, cross the lobby, shake hands, and give each other a hug.

To those who do not recognize either man, they blend with those senior citizens who occasionally drift in from the hot streets to read the complimentary newspapers of the day, or use the bathrooms.

Old guys…

"What goes through their minds?" I want to ask.

Arthur recognizes somebody, and goes to him.

Allan Dwan turns and laughs, "We're still here!"

"So many of those old films were *allowed* to rot," Allan Dwan says. "I suppose we're to blame. It's our own fault. We never thought of saving those early efforts.

"Don't read me wrong, or get the impression that we threw those films away. I mean, we never thought anybody would want to see them again a few months later. They were made for the moment, the weekly moment, the time they were shown, the time people went to see them. It was strictly a *product* for people to see.

"It's because of a lot of collectors that any of our work survived. Studios stored them, and then they made room for newer products.

"That so much has survived is a miracle. A lot of those early films *disintegrated* over time, or because of the advent of sound. Sound, at the end of the silent era, meant progress.

"The phonograph record had a similar history. After 78's came the 45's and the 33 1/3 playing record. The steady sellers, Caruso for example, were more regarded than the popular artist of the moment.

In film, some projectionists or what later became the archivists, took great pains to preserve their treasures. I know some projectionists buried some of these early films in their dirt cellars in an effort to protect them from the sun, because often the sun would cause these films to catch fire. They were always keeping a bucket of water on the floor near the film projector in case of any unexpected fires.

"I'd love to watch Emil Jannings in *Quo Vadis* again, or to watch a set of Ham and Bud comedies (Bud Duncan and Lloyd Hamilton). Jackie Gleason's Poor Soul was nothing more than his take on Lloyd Hamilton.

"Making motion pictures, even in the old days when we and the product were in our infancy and still learning just what the camera could and could not do, was always a funny kind of business.

"In the theatre it was perfectly natural to see something *full stage*, but if you wanted that intimate moment to have an impact on the audience, you had to see it from the point of view of the *eye of the camera*.

"In motion pictures, then and now, there are no balconies. What you watch on the screen in the third row of the orchestra is the same scene you see from the rear of the second balcony.

"The camera, we eventually learned, brings everything *closer*. It thinks for us. It manipulates us, and how *we*, the audience should think.

"But ultimately, the *audience* is still the judge. They *like* it, or they *don't* like it.

"Small gestures lost on stage are magnified with a camera. Griffith showed us that. You can't show feelings in someone's eyes in the theatre. But a camera tells you how the character thinks. That's the difference between a film and a stage play.

"Ignorant studio bosses who were always conscious of the almighty buck would argue, 'People pay to see a whole person, not somebody cut off at the waist.' And Griffith would walk right up to them, look them squarely in the eye, and challenge them, 'Look at me. Do you see my shoes? As you talk to me right now: does it make a difference whether or not you can see my shoes?'

"Griffith, contrary to what Lillian [Gish] says did not invent the close-up. He knew the camera, and the workings of the camera, but he also had the services of a Billy Bitzer.

"When Broncho Billy Anderson, who was G.M. Anderson, born Max Aronson, fired that gun at the end of Edison's *The Great Train Robbery* (1903), that very moment showed the difference between the stage play and the new motion picture that was able to convey emotion to all parts of any theatre without words.

"An intimate visual, and it changed the way a story was told.

"Was *The Great Train Robbery* a good narrative film?

"Yes.

"Well-paced?

"Yes.

"But it was that gunshot, that gunshot, or maybe a wise nickelodeon manager had somebody fire a pistol filled with blanks, that put that little film across.

"And that changed films forever. Watching 30 seconds or a minute of seeing a train leaving the station, or ducks in the lake in the park learning how to follow their mother in the water, or a little baby trying to eat from a cereal bowl by himself: all things of the past.

"Edison himself didn't think highly of the motion picture novelty. I don't think he even took a patent out on his film stock. He thought little of movies except as something illiterate immigrants could possibly like. Pictures, no words. Something to occupy their time, and keep them happy and out of trouble.

"Edwin Porter, who worked for Edison, saw Edison's invention as something else. It was a way to tell stories. It was a way of taking the audience all over the country, maybe even the world, without making them leave their seats.

"But Edison, the businessman, saw motion pictures as a *money drain*.

"Motion pictures meant actors.

"Actors cost money.

"What *respectable* actor would want to give up using his voice and just make gestures which could look ridiculous when magnified by the camera, and shown on the screen?

"And how many times would you have to shoot the same scene?

"In the meantime, there were others who saw a future in making motion pictures that told *stories*, and used *actors*.

"A German immigrant named [Siegfried] Lubin was making films in Philadelphia.

"Most of those so-called actors were people off the street who made a few dollars for a day's work. Some were stage actors out of work, who took the day work with a promise that their name wouldn't be used. To them, the "flickers" were a disgrace, and making them meant you were unable to get legitimate work in the theatre. Most of those early films were good for a week or two. Audiences sat through anything that showed motion.

"Making movies, the handling of movies, changed after *The Great Train Robbery*. Audiences wanted *action*, and a story line they could follow.

"I got into directing because I knew how to instinctively integrate the *action* into the story.

"No long speeches with gestures like rolling your eyes.

"But this was almost a decade after *The Great Train Robbery*.

"I wasn't there at the beginning.

"And neither was [D.W.] Griffith.

"Or [Mack] Sennett.

"Griffith and Sennett were unemployed stage actors who didn't exactly *drift* into motion pictures. They were out of work actors who just didn't want to do any touring with these fly-by-night stock companies who sometimes found themselves abandoned in small towns without any money.

"So they swallowed their dignity and fancy speeches about the *theatre* as the only pure art form, and they took their places in motion pictures, and made, to their amazement, motion picture *history*.

"But don't think they wouldn't have given it up to go back to the New York stage.

"Something had changed their minds: easy money, and available young girls who wanted to be in the movies, whether or not they had any acting talent.

"I was never an actor in the way those men were. I did some stage work at Notre Dame, and I was a football player, but I studied to be an electrical engineer. Anything mechanical fascinated me. I always had a curious mind. I wanted to know things worked—even a motion picture camera.

"I had watched *The Great Train Robbery*, and I knew why it was so popular. It wasn't that gunshot at the end of the film. That was only the icing on the cake.

"I'll tell you who's a great writer: O. Henry. And I still read and re-read two of his stories: *The Gift of the Magi* and *The Furnished Room*. He wrote with a camera's eye for a newspaper audience that didn't have the time or the patience to wade through all of that description.

"He hooked his readers in that opening paragraph the way a director of a one-reeler hooks an audience with good establishing shots.

"We were entertainers who used film instead of words. We told stories with pictures, a series of moving images that were interpreted by the eye of the viewer. We had to turn out enough material for a reel a week.

"Look at O. Henry. He constantly turned out stories. His newspaper audience, and our nickelodeon audience, didn't care about *artistic problems* or things like that. The television audience is the same way. At six o'clock, they want to sit down and watch the six o'clock news. *At six o'clock*. Not earlier, not later.

"The six o'clock news, O. Henry, and the early films were bread-and-butter basics. Those people who sat in those 14th Street nickelodeons came in off the street, and they wanted to see something. They wanted to be entertained. They wanted to see something that wasn't very demanding. Some had an education, many were just working-class folks with a few pennies to plunk down for a few minutes of entertainment. Nothing else. If you wanted to 'educate them,' you had to sneak it in.

"I was an electrical engineer, and my attitude was not very romantic toward the making of a motion picture. It was very workman-like, like the utilization of a formula. The great writers must have had a formula. They were like alchemists who knew how to attract and sustain the interest of various audiences through the years.

"Why does each generation discover something *new* about them?

"Shakespeare's plays easily converted to early filmmaking. His changing scenes, bringing in new characters, are little more than fades and dissolves, and his scenes don't last too long. He should have gone into films. Even without dialogue you know what is going on. Do we have to *hear Romeo and Juliet?*

"In my first efforts, and in the later work I did, I tried to give the audience a good story, to keep my actors moving around to give them something to do, and hopefully hold the interest of the audience.

"The only difference between a one- or two-reeler is how long can that film sustain the interest of an audience. Movies that are too long are nothing more than a stage play that has suddenly become *talky.*

"A novel can go on for pages, and the reader doesn't mind that much. A television audience will walk into the kitchen for a beer. A theatre audience might go to sleep. A movie audience will go for popcorn, *or walk out!*

"Too many yawns aren't very good. In the sound era, they would have 'preview' audiences in remote areas, and give them those sometimes deadly little opinion cards to fill out.

"When I started making motion pictures [1911] we didn't think of those luxuries. We were glad to turn out a reel a week, but we monitored ourselves, and we asked co-workers, 'How does it look?'

"I tried to maintain a set schedule.

"I was reliable. I started on the day I would start, and I finished on the day I said the work would be done.

"I didn't always choose what I wanted to do. Most of my films were assignments. I was told what to do, like a workman in a factory with a product to turn out for a specific market. Those studio heads were business-men, not artists.

"The artists never lasted. The businessmen did. Then and now.

"If you could combine *both*...wow!

"I made all kinds of films: Westerns, dramas, comedies. Some turned out well, some didn't.

"In those early days, you kept on going, and hoped the next one would be better.

"I know you are friends with Lillian [Gish] and I directed *both* of the Gish girls, but I'll tell you something confidentially: Dorothy was the *better*, more versatile actress.

"I know people make the bigger fuss over Lillian, but I think it's because more of her work is available, and has kept on working.

"If you look at her films, one after another, you keep getting the same thing; like James Cagney films - well-executed, but by and large, always the same film.

"Maybe that's what made these people stars. The audience knew what to expect, and they liked what they got.

"In this business, that is all that matters: *they like you.*

"[D.W.]Griffith and [Mack] Sennett's problems were of their own do-ing: they couldn't handle a dollar, and at the end of their lives they were just about broke. Their careers ended before they did.

"Both men lived in hotel rooms. I don't think they ever had their own homes. It's interesting: maybe they couldn't manage on their own, and ho-tel-living does have advantages. Someone makes your bed, etc.

"They were both tragic. Griffith didn't understand *sound* until it was too late, and Sennett was reluctant to make a full-length feature until it was too late.

"Griffith lost Lillian Gish, and Sennett lost Mabel Normand.

"Both ladies saw the handwriting on the wall, and they knew they had to get out. Both men were like fathers who refused to realize their children had grown up.

"Charlie Chaplin knew he had to leave Sennett, too.

"Nothing is constant in this business except work, and the ability to get work.

"You don't say to yourself, 'I know I'm growing.'

"After a certain period, you just look around, and realize you are not the person you were when you started.

"If I were starting out today, I don't know if I'd get into motion pictures. I think I'd get into television, *live* television, if possible, the way it was in the 40's and 50's, when plays and daily soap operas were televised *live*.

"The light goes on, and you just get out there, AND DO IT!"

■

Allan Dwan and Stuart Oderman.

Ann Pennington

1968: NEW YORK: THE HOTEL TIMES SQUARE

What was Ann Pennington to a seasoned theatergoer or nightclub habitue of the twenties and thirties? In one word: everything. The girl with the dimpled knees. The star of several editions of the *Ziegfeld Follies* and *George White's Scandals*, George Gershwin wrote for her. So did Cole Porter and DeSylva, Brown and Henderson. She headlined at the Palace. She introduced the *Black Bottom*.

I mention all of this to her almost half a century later, at the end of the sixties, while she sits against the back of an old, cracked brown leather chair (her feet do not reach the floor; she is barely five feet tall) and closes her eyes momentarily, then suddenly she blinks them open in complete surprise before her head nods and she dozes off.

We are near the West 42nd Street window in the lobby of the Hotel Times Square, a tidy many-floored structure that has not surrendered to the outside urban decay that has slowly and systematically been encroaching upon many areas around the once fabled Times Square.

It is a little after nine o'clock on a snowy pre-Christmas morning in December, 1968, and the snoring of the other white-haired and balding tenants in tattered winter coats is undisturbed and constant amidst the sounds of revolving doors ushering in tourists with their suitcases and cameras.

Outside, the show begins to cover the assorted litter in the streets and remains of broken bottles of the previous evening. The prostitutes now number six. They slap their ungloved hands against the sides of their new leather coats as they line up beneath the torn green awning over a small

49

liquor store next door. Within the hour, the first of a series of policemen in patrol cars will arrive, and they will ask the girls to disperse, or be arrested.

The girls know this often-repeated routine, and they pay it not matter. They will be out and at the same locations the next day. But now, for the sake of their own self-esteem, it is too cold to be standing and waiting.

The hotel lobby is beginning to stir with general early morning hubbub. Vacuum cleaners drone across the rug, and ashtrays are emptied.

Ann Pennington is awake now. She stretches her tiny body, and pats her multicolored woolen tam, making sure the bobby pins are keeping it neatly in place. She looks at her wristwatch and she lifts it to her ear. She peers across the crowded lobby at the elevator.

"I came down real early today," she says cheerfully. "I didn't feel much like sleeping."

She takes tiny steps to the revolving door, motioning to me to follow her.

"It looks cold outside," says. "Is it?"

"It is."

"Is this coat warm enough, do you think?"

"It should be."

She smiles and reaches inside her pockets. "I've got my gloves this time." She holds up a pair of red mittens. "See? All nice and bright for Christmas."

I watch her tug them slowly over her hands. She continues to look outside at the swirling flakes of snow.

"All that cold. I guess it's the right time for it, huh? I almost didn't get to the Automat yesterday. They make nice oatmeal there, but I think they're going to raise the prices on their breakfasts. I hope they don't." She reaches for my arm. "Could you walk me down to Broadway? There's a wind outside, and I don't like winds."

We take tiny steps against the wind. Her breathing is very heavy and forced. I suggest that we head back to the hotel, and perhaps leave an hour later. She shakes her head, and we continue walking.

"You know, I don't care about a lot of that stuff you talked about last week. That's all in the past. And I don't like to think about it. You know what it all adds up to? A lot of lights, and sometimes a lot of money. That's all this business is. Sometimes one covers for the other. Sometimes, if you are lucky, you get both."

Ann Pennington.

She pats the tam, and starts to enter the Automat. "Thanks for walking me. I guess my friend didn't show up today, so I'll eat alone. Don't you catch cold, and good luck with your piano playing.

"Can I talk about you on the Joe Franklin show," I start to ask. "I'll be taping…"

She shrugs her shoulders, and disappears inside.

Several days pass. My note to her is unanswered. She doesn't even return my telephone calls, even collect.

"You broke your promise," she says when she sees me coming out of the path of the revolving door. She is wearing no makeup at ten in the morning and her face looks tired. "You talked about me on that television show. I told you I don't like it. I once heard my name on the Carson show. I don't want people coming after me, and bothering me. Let them remember me as I was when I was younger…What is that thing under your arm?"

I hand her the long white box which contains a single red rose. Like a child she grabs it, tears away the wrapping, and holds up the flower. "These hotel clerks don't know a thing about me. They don't know anything about me. They just watch the clock until it's time to go."

I bring out a photograph. It is on thick paper: a picture of a young girl, perhaps fifteen or sixteen years old. She is wearing a full-length white dress and she is smiling. She is sitting, properly posed, on a small sofa.

She looks at the picture, her eyes closing, trying to place it in time. "That's a Sunday school dress," she says, opening her eyes. "I think I wore it in *Susie Snowflake* (1916), my *first* film. My *very* first film."

Now she is smiling. "You wouldn't have any other pictures with you?" Her eyes are bright with pride.

"No," I slowly answer, "but I could make a copy…"

She doesn't let me finish. Her face is dull again, the light out of her eyes, as when I entered the lobby. "I'm not really interested in that old stuff. I was just thinking…I mean that picture of me isn't what you would call a typical pose. You know I started when I was pretty young…"

She was born in Wilmington, Delaware on December 23, 1893. Her first New York appearance was at the Astor Theatre on November 6, 1911, in a production of *The Red Window*.

"…and we were living in Camden, New Jersey. My father was with the Victor people, so we always had plenty of music in the house. My teacher used to send some of us to the Keith and Proctors Vaudeville Theatre in Philadelphia, which was not too far away. They put on little shows and we had small parts. My mother used to take me, and one night I was seen by Carter DeHaven's mother, and she gave me a part in the chorus…"

A few minutes pass. My photograph is still on her lap. Now she reaches for the *Daily News*, which a clerk has sent to her.

"Yes?" she asks, as if I were somebody she is meeting for the first time.

I point to the photograph. "You have my picture."

She looks at me accusingly. "I'll sign it for you."

I hand her a felt-tipped pen, and she writes slowly across the old surface. *To Stuart. Best. Ann Pennington.*

"What happened after you left Philadelphia?"

She pushes the picture at me, and reaches down for the newspaper. "I don't know anything about Philadelphia. And I'm not going to talk about Philadelphia. It's all over anyway. You can't keep thinking and talking about what you did a long time ago…Thanks for the flower, and don't talk about me on that television show."

I left her, and headed for the studio.

The following evening I had dinner at George Olsen's restaurant in Paramus, New Jersey. In the twenties, Olsen's orchestra had appeared in several stage hits: *Kid Boots* (the Ziegfeld show starring Eddie Cantor), Rodgers and Hart's *The Girl Friend*, Jerome Kern's *Sunny*, and DeSylva, Brown, and Henderson's collegiate *Good News*.

"I knew Ann when she first came to New York," George Olsen tells me, laughing at the signed photo. "Penny must have been in her teens because many years later we did a picture together (*Happy Days*, 1929). She was a hard working girl, and hadn't appeared in the *Follies* or the *Scandals* yet. I was the drummer in the pit band and she was up there on the stage shaking around to 'The World is Waiting for the Sunrise.' You couldn't go near her with her mother hanging around all the time as chaperon, and Penny was kind of shy anyway; she was a cute little girl. Fresh and snappy, and very tiny." He whispers the next few words. "She's not in good straits, is she?"

"She was an okay girl as long as her mother was around. She managed Penny's money, but Penny wanted to be on her own like a lot of those girls. A lot of those Follies girls made big money, but they couldn't handle it. All of that fast life.

"Some of them married wealthy guys or got out while they were still young. And some of them got mixed up with crooked agents, and wound up owing them money. And some of them ran with gangsters and kept it quiet until it got out of hand.

"Penny was always involved with somebody and newspapers were always writing about it. She was always engaged and getting married.

"But she never got married.

"If you want to know what hurt Penny the most, it was the ponies. She loved to go to the track. You couldn't keep her away from it.

"She did a lot of shows. She had good bookings, and bad bookings, but she honored her contracts, and she worked for years. And then," he snaps his fingers, "boom! All finished. Gone! Not a word about her!

"But that's how it is in this business. You do your shows and go home and mind how you live."

In the summer I am playing for a series of silent film showings in Los Angeles at the Masquers, a theatrical clubhouse, whose walls are lined with framed caricatures of Walter Catlett, Joe Penner, Eddie Cantor, Clark and McCullough, Joe E. Brown, Ed Wynn, Harry Langdon, Alan Mowbray, Cary Grant…

And the members tell good stories about the early days.

"Penny liked to dance, and she liked going to nightclubs," one of the Masquers tells me. "She liked the clubs in Harlem where the music was a little jumpier and the atmosphere was less formal. She could really move around and a lot of the best dancing and music was done after hours. She was pretty free with her money, always giving it to who asked her, and I don't think a lot of them ever paid her back. And she was too shy to remind them. You know the Fanny Brice story, don't you?

"They did a few shows together (The *Follies* of 1916, 1917, and 1923).

"This isn't a theatre story. It's about an incident involving Nick Arnstein, Fanny's husband. He was a good-looking guy and a gambler, and he was always in a lot of trouble.

"Fanny knew this, and she was always prepared for those kinds of emergencies. She always had a lot of extra dough around the house in the most unexpected places.

"This time she was really stuck. The judge set a high bail, and even Fanny didn't have that much money. She didn't want Nick spending the night in jail. I guess she knew he wouldn't be too safe there.

"So she took a chance and called Penny late at night, and Penny came over with a bundled scarf and twenty-thousand dollars worth of jewelry. It was one of the few times Fanny ever asked for help.

"Fanny never forgot it was Penny who helped her.

"Penny had a long career as dancers go, and for the kind of dancing she did. But when it came to an end, she had no money to speak of, and no husband, and no family.

"Fanny went into radio as Baby Snooks, and when Fanny heard about Penny, she asked her to come to California and stay with her as a house guest and maybe get some character parts in movies. Sidekick roles, like

Patsy Kelly used to play.

"Fanny took her everywhere: producer's parties, luncheons. She even bought her some clothes, but she took the labels off, and pretended they were old and used when she gave them to her.

"You know who could tell you Penny stories? Harry Richman. He lives in Santa Monica near the beach."

Harry Richman's bungalow is less than a half-mile away from the Santa Monica Holiday Inn where I am staying. You wouldn't think the former King of Broadway and Ziegfeld star of 1931 to be living in such modest surroundings.

"For my time of life," he explains as I enter, "this is good enough. Even in the old days when I was working with Helen Morgan and Ruth Etting, you could only be in one room at a time." He laughs and points to several signed photographs of Clara Bow and Jean Harlow, and Lenore Ulric that are crowded together atop his grand piano. "I knew them all, and very well," he smiles wistfully.

"I went through a lot of money," he continues, and my eyes are directed to a scrapbook on the coffee table. The scrapbook is opened to a set of reviews, yellowed with age, from an old engagement at the Cafe de Paris in London. "I went through a lot of women. I played women the way Penny played horses. I'd *still* be chasing the women, but they don't hang around the two-dollar window. I'm trying to get producers interested in my life story. Be a good thing for Sinatra. Tell Penny I'll give her a role."

Back in New York I remind Ann Pennington of her *Ziegfeld Follies* debut at the Amsterdam Theatre on June 16, 1923.

"Stuart, you know this street wasn't like this then. Forty-second Street was very respectable, and when you went to the theatre, you wore your best clothes. Women wore long gowns, and men wore tuxedos."

"What was Leon Errol like to work with?" I ask.

"Leon was very funny when he was onstage, and he was very serious when he was off-stage, like a lot of comedians. He never ad-libbed his lines. He rehearsed with Bert Williams, who was a gentleman, Leon did a rubber legs routine. You know, pretending to fall down. He'd rehearse these dance steps with one girl all day, over and over again, making sure she got everything right. But at night he'd do a different set of steps, and the poor girl would fall all over his feet trying to follow him. What made the routine work night after night was Leon's telling her to keep a straight face and not break up. To get that laugh, the girl had to be stately looking and totally composed at all times.

"Ziegfeld didn't the idea of the audiences laughing at his girls unless they were comediennes like Fanny Brice. He argued with Leon several times, but Leon always had the same answer: you get your laughs by doing the unexpected.

"Ziegfeld didn't feel at home or at ease with comedians. He was always afraid of being laughed at behind his back, or that a dig would be written into one of the monologues at a performance he didn't attend. A lot of the comics became famous because of the *Follies*: Ed Wynn, Eddie Cantor, and W.C. Fields, but Ziegfeld wanted them onstage for only a short time.

"What did he consider a short time?

"Long enough for the girls to change for the next song or production number.

"He liked Will Rogers. Rogers used to walk on stage with his lariat and do a few tricks, and then put the lariat down and talk about the news of the day, and give opinions about things he read in the papers. Since the papers changed everyday, no two performances were exactly alike. He didn't do sketches like Cantor or Fields. Those two loved sketches because they could be physical, but Will Rogers just stood and talked. I don't know if he stayed on longer than the other comedians, but he easily could have turned his turn into an Evening, if he thought the audience had warmed up to the routine.

"But he never did that, no matter how much the audience screamed for him. He knew he was part of a revue, and he knew it was smarter to leave them wanting more.

"Ziegfeld didn't like a lot of his performers personally, but he knew talent when he saw it, and that was what really mattered to him the most. He had great respect for Will Rogers and he never gave him a *written* contract. Everything was agreed to on a handshake: salary, billing, everything. And Ziegfeld paid *him* at the right time.

I ask, "Are you hinting that Ziegfeld used to avoid paying his people on payday?"

Her answer is a loud laugh.

When I go to visit her the following week, she isn't in the lobby.

The clerk at the front desk says she went to the track a few hours ago.

Am I from the Relief Board? It is the first time someone has officially told me she has been living on welfare.

The stars with whom Ann Pennington appeared in the *Follies* editions from 1913 to 1918 are a veritable Who's Who of the American theatre.

"I worked with Imogene Wilson," she says, looking at a collection of photographs. "Imogene Wilson was her name when she was in the *Follies* but she changed it to Mary Nolan when she went to Hollywood.

"A sad girl. A real sad girl. You know there are some people who have everything, and make it turn out real rotten? That was Imogene's problem. Men. She always got herself into bad situations. She was sweet on a comedian named Frank Tinney, but he was married, and he'd never divorce his wife.

"Frank Tinney used to beat her up. She'd come into the theatre all braised and battered, and tell us she'd had a bad fall. If it were wintertime, she'd tell us she slipped on the ice.

"I think Prank wasn't the only man who beat her up. There were others. She was kind of crazy that way, if you know what I mean. Even when she went to Hollywood she was the same old Imogene Wilson men could beat up. I guess she liked being punched around."

"What was it like, being a Follies girl?" I ask.

"It was a job," she answers.

"Is that all?"

"That's all it ever was. That's all this business is. That's all it ever was. After you put in your time studying and watching other performers, you hope someone is willing to take a chance on you. People don't understand that kind of talk from performers, but that's the honest truth of it. You're either working or you're not working, and as far as the glamour is concerned, there are shows you like, and shows you don't like.

"Chorus girls got seventy-five dollars a week, and that was pretty good money for those days. Most of the girls in the other shows got around forty. If you worked for Ziegfeld, you knew you were better than the other girls.

"Mr. Ziegfeld had *rules*. You had to dress *just so*, look *just so*, and behave properly in restaurants. That was the glamour part, and I think the girls were paid extra money to buy good clothes."

I ask, "How did Ziegfeld girls like Hope Dare and Lilyan Tashman achieve prominence?"

Ann Pennington fingers the bobby pins underneath her tam. The question clearly confuses her. How do you account for someone else's success?

"Those two weren't *exactly* chorus girls. They were showgirls. They were taller than the chorus girls, and they had that certain look. And that's what Ziegfeld liked: that certain look. I can't describe it, but you know it when you see it. And those ladies had it, and if you have it, anything is possible.

"If Ziegfeld had any real competition, it was probably George White, who produced the *Scandals*. He used to dance for Ziegfeld. George also had a good eye for talent. He hired a young kid named George Gershwin to write the music, Alfred Newman, who became a Hollywood composer, to conduct the orchestra, and yours truly.

"George Gershwin *loved* to play the piano, especially his own music. He was a natural pianist, and he had good technique, and he played with great assurance and self-confidence. He was the rehearsal pianist. He liked the show business of it all.

"Cole Porter, who did some writing for me, was very shy. He didn't play the piano very well, and he would never play for singers or rehearsals the way George did. George was a natural born salesman, always grinning and saying, 'Here are the songs. I *know* you'll like them.' And Porter would say, 'Here are the songs. I *hope* you'll like them.'"

She shrugs her shoulders and laughs. "It doesn't really matter what composers are like at rehearsals anyway. What really counts is the audience, and I think those boys did okay, don't you?"

Throughout all of our early morning conversations and meetings, the talk is always concentrated on the theatre. Ann is a stage person, and she tells me movies don't really mean that much to stage people.

"If a person ever did a movie at that time, it was strictly for the money. I did a few films: talkies and silents, but I would rather work in a theatre to live people, not a bunch of cameras. Movies take too much time. It takes all day to get a few good usable minutes, and for dancers movies are terrible. A dancer likes to keep dancing, and they get tired after all of those takes. And movies make you look heavier. Those old movies were big on showing fat thighs and stuff.

"I didn't do any big parts in films. I played dancing parts. Sometimes I played a man's last fling before he got married, but I was always a dancer. I frankly never understood why, before he got married, a man would want to have a fling with a chorus girl. Those plots never made sense."

I ask, "Didn't rich men chase Ziegfeld girls? I read in old newspapers about bankers and…"

"Stuart, being courted and being chased are two different things. We were pretty expensive girls, but," she says very softly, "we were very nice and wholesome. We never took advantage of any man who did not show us the jewelry first. If he came backstage with diamonds, it was every girl for herself. A lot of those girls had collections of both men and diamonds. It's okay if you know how to handle it, I guess.

"I don't go along with this Women's Lib. Stuart, honey, any woman can get whatever she wants out of any man. All she has to do is treat him kindly. Once she does that…anything."

"Do you remember a film called *Manhandled*?"

She nods, "That was a Famous Players production with Gloria Swanson. I'm in the party sequence with Brooke Johns and Lilyan Tashman. That was filmed right here in New York. I was doing a *Follies* with Brooke Johns. Brooke and I went into the *Follies* right after *Jack and Jill*."

I ask nothing about Brooke Johns to whom she was once engaged, and called "an item" by the columnists. Like her other publicized engagements, it fell through. Ann never married.

"I'm in only one sequence in *Manhandled*. Have you ever seen any films with Lilyan Tashman? She was so beautiful. Tall. Blonde. Very patrician looking. She had an expensive wardrobe, and she died so terribly young. Maybe she was thirty-five. She was married to Eddie Lowe, and she was the one real love of his life."

"Do you remember a film called *The Mad Dancer*?"

She nods. "It was the one film I had the lead in, a *real* lead. I played a girl who danced in the Latin Quarter of Paris, and the picture created a scandal because there was a nude statue of me. They gave me more *acting* to do, which was okay with me. I don't know why I was never given any dramatic roles."

"One of your films, *Pretty Ladies*, co-starred Lucille LeSeuer," I begin.

"Lucille changed her name to Joan Crawford, and when she became famous, the studio tried to cash in on that early film. The *real* star was Lilyan Tashman. We did *Gold Diggers of Broadway* together. Nick Lucas and Winnie Lightner were in it, too. Nick did that 'Tip Toe Through the Tulips' number, and I did 'Painting the Clouds With Sunshine,' which had color tints."

As if on cue, she sits up on the cracked brown leather chair, and starts to sing-whisper a few measures. Except for the constant tapping of her hand on the side of the chair, there is no accompaniment. A few measures later, she looks around and sees almost an empty lobby. Now her body starts to sway and her foot starts to move on the floral rug. At the end of the song she stands up and does a quick time-step, reaching for my hand. She is breathless.

The sky outside is ashen. A liquor bottle is hurled against the sidewalk. As it shatters, a police car rounds the corner, and the prostitutes scatter in all directions.

"You know what the problem was," Ann says, her breathing becoming normal again. "I was only a dancer, and I don't dance anymore. I don't do anything anymore except get up and come down here and see who's here. You want to go for a walk to Broadway with me?"

She buttons her coat, and reaches for my arm. "Come on. Walk with me. You got nothing better to do."

For several minutes nothing is said. She clutches my arm tightly. "Do I look okay?"

The Automat is a world of brown marble, and a constant clattering of silverware and crockery. A line of elderly people with nowhere to go stand holding their brown plastic trays and paper napkins. There was a time when people would have stood on line to see Ann. Now the situation is reversed.

"They didn't know how to work with sound in those days," she says, as the line presses forward. "The microphone was all they cared about. You could have people sit in a chair for five or ten minutes like Janet Gaynor did, and nobody minded. If the sound was clear, everything was okay.

"It was rough on dancers. How do you think a chorus line of tap dancers sounded? And then add the singing. My God, it was noisy. And you couldn't take too many close-ups of people dancing because the camera made too much noise.

"I would have loved to play dramatic parts. Character roles. But they never gave me a chance. To the studio heads, I was a Follies girl, and I was typed as soon as they signed me up.

"Wait a minute! I did do one character part, but it didn't amount to much. It was in a George Montgomery film. *China...*something or other.

It was right after a stage version *Student Prince*. I spoke a few lines in one scene, but I was still a dancer. Maybe you'd call it a hostess."

She squeezes my hand and disappears into the line, I wonder if the people at the serving tables or on line know who she is.

Or do they know who she is, and are they wondering who I am...

After the run of *George White's Scandals of 1928*, Ann goes to Hollywood and is busy in five successive films: *Happy Days*, *Is Everybody Happy?*, *Night Parade*, and *Pretty Ladies*. The parts are obvious: a resort entertainer, a *Follies* girl, and a dancer who happens to be in the same room when the leading man asks, "Have you seen her? She's in a show right here in town!"

Nineteen thirty-one marks Penny's eighteenth year of continuous Broadway work, save for a motion picture stint. Nine editions of the *Follies*, four *Scandals*, three musicals, and a few weeks as a vaudeville headliner at the Palace.

Eager for any kind of work, she accepts a job co-starring in *Stars and Strips*, a Chicago burlesque revue which features Rosita Royce, a stripper whose trained pigeons are a necessary part of the act. By the tone of the Chicago newspapers, this engagement is a big step-down.

"I never understood the controversy," Penny recalls. "All I did was take an available job during the Depression. I did the same kind of dancing I had been doing for years. I didn't do any of the bumps and grinds the other girls did. Mine was a solo turn."

Over the next seven years, she appeared in touring productions of musicals, limited engagements in Brooklyn, and a long engagement at the Club Paradise, a New York nightclub run under the supervision of George White, to whom she was once engaged.

She sums it up very quickly for me. "You go where the work is. If you don't like it, quit.

She returns to the Broadway stage in a revival of Romberg's *Student Prince* in a character part, a supporting role which should have led to other character parts and supporting roles. She is approaching fifty, too old to compete with the jitterbuggers, but certainly old enough to do the type of role Billie Burke is doing so successfully in films.

What she hopes for does not materialize. With the exception of a surprise appearance at a 1946 show business benefit, she is not seen on the stage or screen ever again.

"If you're looking for Miss Pennington, she's not coming out of her room today," one of the guests tells me. "I knocked on the door a few times and I told her everything was safe, but she didn't answer. Her television set is playing real low, so I know she can get out of bed. She's been eating a few sandwich cookies she keeps in a box on the window sill."

He adjusts his eyeglasses and digs his worn shoes into the rug. "Rotten dogs! That's all this city is! Anybody with half a brain could see she wasn't carrying any pocketbook or handbag. She was walking back from the Automat, and they mugged her by the newspaper trucks. They don't have any streetlights there."

I rush to the telephones and buzz her room. Once. Twice. A third time. No answer.

Three weeks later. Early summer. One of the first hot days.

She is sitting in the cracked leather chair by the window. Her breathing is erratic and forced. She has lost a considerable amount of weight, and the sleeves of her red blouse droop at the shoulders. Her left cheek is badly bruised and during the first few minutes of conversation she pretends to be shielding herself from the sun, and the glances of anyone outside by turning her face away.

"It's not my New York anymore," she quietly says. "It's not my town. I used to keep crazy hours all over this city. Times Square. Sheridan Square. Harlem. And nothing ever happened to me. And then, a few weeks ago: boom! I don't know how I ever got back to the hotel. I think the word is stumbled back, right?

"In the old days I used to go to breakfast without even going to bed. I was a real Manhattan baby. *Now* I sleep a lot. I think nature is catching up on me. Play when you're young. Sleep when you're old…When are you leaving for California?"

"At the end of the week," I answer. "That's why I stopped by."

She shakes her head. "You came by twice when I was upstairs, and you left me some groceries. I knew they came from you before I read the note. Can I say something to you, Stuart? You don't comb your hair right."

It isn't what I expected to hear, and I quickly touch the top of my head.

"You feel that space? I saw it the last time you were on television. Can I comb your hair for you?"

She stands up and pretends to yank me to a full-length mirror near the mailbox.

"Tilt your head to me," she says. "I'm pressing down your hair with the flat of the comb. You'll look like *The Patent Leather Kid*, but while you're under the lights you'll look like a headliner."

She kisses me quickly on the cheek, and gives my hand an additional squeeze. "And take care of yourself in California. A lot of the people I knew aren't there anymore, but say hello to the ones who are."

When I am outside the hotel, she is standing at the window and waving to me.

I broke my promise. I didn't visit her when I came back from California. I sent postcards from shore resorts and from small New Jersey towns. When I visited the hotel in late-October it was too late.

The cracked leather chair she always occupied was no longer by the window. Someone had pushed it to the far end of the lobby, and turned it upside down.

"She's not here," yells someone across the silence of the lobby. "She's in Brooklyn."

He doesn't say anything more. Maybe he thinks I know the full story.

"Way out in Brooklyn," he yells again and crosses over to the front window. "It's a two-hour trip. I went to see her three days ago, and I spent an hour with her. She didn't know I was in the same room. They've got her all wired up with tubes and machines. I couldn't find a place to sit down. She talked about Chicago. She doesn't want to go there anymore."

He laughs. "She must think she's on the stage when she says that, right? I guess once you're a show business celebrity…"

"What happened to her?" I ask.

"And she was in such good condition last week, too. Joking and laughing in the elevator…"

Silence. He looks down at his shoes, and then he looks up at me. His smile is gone, and his expression is blank. "She just couldn't go on anymore. She just couldn't go on anymore."

I don't go to visit her, and I don't send flowers or a get-well card. I send a postcard I brought back from Santa Monica. *I was here. Love…*

She died at Beekman Downtown Hospital on November 4, 1971. I don't know if anyone was there.

The *New York Times* obituary column headlines her passing as Ann Pennington, Dancing Star, but, as one reads the column, her life after the early forties becomes progressively bleaker, and the truth, *her* truth, and show business clichés, become pathetically intertwined. What emerges in the final paragraphs seems almost out of *Sister Carrie*.

"...years of living alone in a small room in a side street hotel off Broadway. Toward the end she appeared to be living in the past, moving slowly along the Broadway where once her name had been in blazing lights."

I can't argue or find fault with the sentence that follows: "There are no known survivors..."

■

Dorothy Davenport
(Mrs. Wallace) Reid

AUGUST 1975: LOS ANGELES: THE HOLLYWOOD
ROOSEVELT HOTEL

A few minutes before the meeting room is filled to capacity with folding chairs, I hastily remove the assortment of empty beer bottles still on top of an old, out-of-tune piano, a hold over from the previous function whose participants had neither concern nor care regarding the condition of the room. Obviously the piano wasn't used. In some hotels in colder parts of the country, the piano would have been covered with coats.

"You're an artist," someone says behind me. "You shouldn't have to carry out trash before a performance. Do you have a dressing room? You should have asked for one, even if you only stay there for a few minutes to see people, and thank them. There are very few rewards in this business. Courtesy should not be a bonus. It should be an automatic given."

The speaker is Dorothy Davenport, whose career in motion pictures began as a horseback rider in westerns made by David Horsley's "wash-tub-and-sink" Centaur Studio in Bayonne, New Jersey in 1911. Horsley's film, *Desperate Desmond*, written by *New York Journal* writer Harry Hershfeld, later known for his *Can You Top This?* radio series, would send Hershfeld and Dorothy Davenport to Los Angeles the following year.

Dorothy waves at a tall middle-aged man headed in our direction. "My son," she tells me. "Wallace Reid, Jr. It's nice to say Wally's name, and have a Wally here to hear it."

Her voice is deep and full. Every sound is clearly enunciated, a sign of being trained to project to the very last rows of the theatre when she was touring in stock companies. In the 1970's she still appears onstage, but usually at senior citizens' centers where she reads the news aloud to interested listeners.

Mrs. Wallace Reid, as she usually refers to herself since the death of her husband (born William Wallace Reid) in 1923 at the age of 31, sits next to her son in the front row near the piano.

The meeting room has been filling up. Directors Allan Dwan and David Butler enter at the same time. Following are actors Ben Lyon, Marian Nixon (whom he married after the death of Bebe Daniels), Richard Arlen, and Jack Oakie.

Each is applauded. Nobody has to wear an identifying name tag. This is a *silent film* audience. They not only know who is who, but when to laugh, and when to shed a tear during showings of their films.

Almost sixty years old, William Wallace Reid, Jr. sits wonder-eyed as the child he was when his father passed away. "I barely knew him," he whispers as Dwan, Oakie, and Arlen give his mother a hug or a sign of recognition. "I have photographs of him holding me as a child, but to see him on the big screen…This crowd knows more about my dad than I do. I'm older than he was when he made these films. *Much older*…The child is the father of the man."

"I'll tell you about Wally," Dorothy says when we are alone after a showing of clips from *The Affairs of Anatol*, a Paramount-DeMille film starring Wally and Gloria Swanson. "He was a good man, and we had a good, strong marriage, and we stayed married until he died. Not too many Hollywood couples, then or now, can say that. This is an industry that gives marriages and divorces as much publicity as its motion pictures. This is an industry that prides itself on beauty. Just go on the beaches, and you'll see what I mean. Every girl who gets off the bus thinks she is going to sit by the water in a revealing swimsuit and be discovered…

"Beauty lasts so long, and then it's over. Or else you just keep hanging on, and play *mothers*. Or maybe an older neighbor, who makes wisecracks.

"Rita Hayworth couldn't make the adjustment. She couldn't allow herself to age with her audience. I remember when she was playing support to Joan Crawford. Joan Crawford was smart. She knew she couldn't dance a Charleston on a tabletop forever. She knew instinctively how to age. Jeff Chandler had a great love scene with her decades later in *Female on the Beach*. Jeff Chandler had the gray hair. Joan didn't.

"This is a tough town, and even the toughest don't survive without scars. I knew when you saw me what you were thinking. And that was the same question I was thinking: What can I ask you about Wally? Is it okay?

"I don't mind. You have a little more interest in these films because you've been playing for them, and who knows if we'll ever meet again?

"We weren't faces hired off the street. The Davenports and the Reids were *of the theatre*. My father [Harry Davenport: 1866-1949] was the doctor in *Gone With the Wind* and my mother [Alice] and my sisters [Ann and Kate] worked for Keystone which is how I know Minta [Durfee, Roscoe 'Fatty' Arbuckle's first wife]. Minta and my mother were in Charlie's [Chaplin] first film, *Making a Living* [1914].

"If you toured in stock and *then* went into films, you brought a little extra something besides a face. You could do scenes, and handle lines. You hoped what looked natural in the theatre didn't register on the big screen as something grotesque.

"Just watch Chaplin's first film with my mother. The poor man was lost. Mack [Sennett] and Mabel [Normand] had just seen him doing a vaudeville turn a few nights earlier, and they loved him. But on the screen…Charlie was almost fired, but wonderful Mabel fought for him, and told Mack that Charlie had great potential.

"Wally could do comedy, but not the type Charlie did. Charlie was physical. Charlie also played a character: a *tramp*. Wally's humor was gentler. He was a real matinee idol, who could play in a period piece as easily as he could be in something contemporary.

"There were always rumors about Wally having romances on the set. I expected that. He was a *man*, a *real* man, and a lot of girls, young girls, were attracted to him. He did gymnastics, and if you see him in those brief scenes in *The Birth of a Nation*, you knew why there was such a strong reaction from the ladies.

"If the stars of any era, silent or sound, had as many romances or affairs as were reported in the newspapers and movie magazines, they wouldn't have the time or the strength to stand in front of a camera!

"You made a reel a week, if you did serials or comedies. Features took a few weeks, sometimes a month, sometimes two. You worked on a predetermined schedule, like you were on an assembly line in a shoe factory. So many shoes, so many feet of film.

"You had to deliver a product on time. Otherwise the theater took other films, and you lost out. If that happened too frequently, you were considered unreliable, which is the worst thing you could say about anybody in those days. The studio head, the producer, the director, the publicity department: they all had to explain what the problem was. If you lost your popularity, it went back *up* the ladder: the publicity department, the director, the producer, the studio head. The public was very fickle. Neighborhood theatres changed their films twice a week for the lesser pictures, the programmers.

"The fan magazines placed us on Mount Olympus, and we had to maintain our image. Your life wasn't your own. Everything you did was chosen for you, and subject to their approval: *what* you wore away from the studio, *whom* you married, had to be given studio approval and how it would affect your returns at the box-office, and where you were seen when dining out."

Wallace Reid had a history of off-screen addiction to narcotics. Amongst the more adventurous personalities, rumors of marijuana and cocaine parties behind closed doors were rampant. Drugs and addiction were not easily discussed by the daily newspapers, or at the dinner tables in the United States.

During the filming of one of the DeMille epics, Reed accidentally stepped on a rusty nail.

Choreographer Agnes DeMille, daughter of director William, and niece of director Cecil B., explained, "My uncle knew what had happened, but he had a doctor there, as he always did, because of the insurance policies on those stars, and as protection against any unforeseen accidents and lawsuits.

"I'm sure there was some pain, but nobody needed to worry about it. Accidents took place all the time, and were taken care of immediately, and the shooting resumed. There was no need to send dozens of people home. The doctor was there to quickly administer an injection of morphine.

"Wally returned to the set after an hour or so, and the whole thing seemed like a short break. I think they were shooting *The Affairs of Anatol* with Gloria Swanson. It was an expensive picture, and Wally wasn't really very well.

"The next day Wally had another dose of pain, and another dose of morphine was given. The pattern was now established: pain, morphine, pain, morphine. Before the film's final shooting days, Wally's morphine addiction was well-known around the Paramount lot.

"Paramount sent Wally to a *private* sanitarium, and no news was released.

"The so-called private sanitarium really was the bottom floor of one of the hospitals. In the basement there were padded rooms adjacent to one another. Each room had a single light burned overhead constantly, a sink, a toilet without a seat, and a small mattress on the floor.

"In this confined space Wally was to cure himself. A doctor, I was told, looked at him from time to time over the next few weeks he was there, but the reports he sent were very general. Nothing specific. The doctor was only there to make sure Paramount's major investment was still alive, and would be able to return to work as soon as possible.

"A nurse would leave food only after Wally had spent the first three days virtually all alone. The food was very soft.

"All of the patients undergoing the same treatment as Wally vomited, urinated, and defecated on themselves and on the floor. Only if the patient were deemed safe would anyone venture inside with a mop and a new hospital gown. Most of the patients stayed naked because they sometimes tore their gowns in anguish.

"Everything was done in secrecy. I wasn't allowed to see him. If someone from Paramount saw him, it was strictly business. *Their* business, not mine.

"If Wally cried out for me, I never knew it...

"He went back to work eventually, but he couldn't function without those morphine shots, and he had to return to that hospital, and go through that whole agonizing process again...

"On one of his visits, I don't think anybody looked at him. No doctors. No nurses. Nobody...

"The first three days were always the same, and he had no other choice but to endure it.

"There were all sorts of rumors regarding the way he died, but I don't want to repeat them. Some say he kept hitting his head against the padded wall. Some say he was just given another dose of morphine just to stop the screaming.

"I always felt that once he was determined to be of no further value, Paramount and DeMille simply forgot about him, and cast him off.

"According to the newspapers of the day, Wally's death was due to lung and kidney congestion. He had lost, during his stay of a few weeks, sixty pounds, dropping down to a weight of 125 pounds. He was six feet tall."

Arrested for violating the Harrison Anti-Narcotic Act were the manager of the private sanitarium, and its owner. In the following years Mrs. Reid became well-known for her campaign to increase public awareness of the dangers of narcotics addiction.

Fifty-two years after her husband's tragic death, she rose from her front row seat at the Hollywood Roosevelt and quietly whispered, "Thank you for Wally, my children, and my grandchildren, and myself. It's good to see Wally on a screen one more time."

■

Billie Rhodes

1968: LABOR DAY: THE HOLLYWOOD ROOSEVELT HOTEL.
We are herded, like galley slaves in Francis X. Bushman's *Ben Hur*, and Milton Sills' *The Sea Hawk*, into one of the banquet rooms, whose walls have been sprayed to the color of an overripe cantaloupe, and the floors have been waxed to an unnatural sheen that never existed in the halcyon days of Vernon and Irene Castle.

After you stop blinking and rubbing your eyes, and begin to take smaller steps, you begin to realize the air-conditioning is faulty, and the last minute installations of two gigantic floor fans at opposite ends of the room do not accomplish much in the effort to alleviate the cramped conditions and the problem of breathing. Hopefully the dinner won't last more than ninety minutes.

The guests of honor are in the same room with us: silent film stars, former directors, stuntmen and cameramen. Wisely they are scattered amongst the tables. One personality per table. Their name tags identify them for us: Minta Durfee Arbuckle, Claire Windsor, Leo G. Carroll, Betty Bronson, Johnny Hines, and Lita Grey Chaplin.

Billie Rhodes is seated at my table. The years have been more than kind to her. It is hard to believe that the date of her first released film is September, 1913. Still petite, her brown hair has few streaks of gray. She is elegantly dressed in black, but what attracts and holds you are her eyes: they are like great brown saucers. The camera loved them. Now these eyes quickly scan the banquet room.

"I haven't seen some of these people in years," she says, "Doesn't Betty Bronson look wonderful?"

Billie reaches for a dinner roll, and there is a moment of silence. I want to have something to talk about besides how wilted the celery looks or where did the waiter go when we asked him to please refill out glasses of water. Even the ice cubes have melted, and what fluid is at the bottom of the glass tastes alien and metallic.

"Was *Two Cylinder Courtship* the film you would have chosen to be shown this afternoon?"

"No," she answers, "but that seems to be the one that always keeps cropping up. Try to catch *Mary's Merry Mix-Up*. They filmed parts of it right at the beach at Santa Monica.

"I'm not in pictures anymore, which is why I'm *not* wearing a nametag. In my day, if you weren't known, you just weren't known. Wearing a nametag won't make any difference. Nobody is going to get any work from this evening, and I frankly came just to watch old movies, and have a good time like a tourist. I don't want to be *on*. I did all that a long time ago, and I *left* it. I knew when it was time to leave, before it left me."

From the podium she hears her name announced. She rises and waves to the direction of the applause and then quickly sits.

"When are they going to start serving?" she asks.

Since that initial meeting, our paths kept crossing: silent film evenings at the Masquers, performances at the Screen Directors Guild, and at parties hosted by Billie's niece, Jean Miller, award-winning producer of *Billie*, a documentary on the life and times of her famous aunt. While the other guests are either milling about or going back for seconds and thirds on the platters from a Fairfax Avenue delicatessen, Billie and I sneak over to the piano. She sings "Oh, You Beautiful Doll" in the key of C, and "Baby Face" in A flat.

"I don't like to give them too much when it's informal. After all, it's only a living room. When I was in vaudeville, I knew when it was time to get off. Some performers stay on for *years*, but a *good* performer knows to leave them wanting for more.

"I was doing vaudeville in San Francisco when I eleven. I was a single, which means I worked alone. The act was only six minutes: two songs separated by a dance and that was it. I could pass for sixteen, if you know what I mean. I may have looked 'old,' but I never traveled alone. My older sister was my chaperone.

"Don't get the impression I was a wise kid trying to be a show business babe. I had been taking singing lessons and dancing lessons, and

Billie Rhodes.

dramatic lessons. I could do Shakespeare, and project my voice all the way up to the balcony. That's the way they taught you diction and clarity in those days. Project all the way up to the balcony.

"I didn't have an agent. I just went backstage, and asked to speak to the manager. His name was Ben Lust. A nice man. He asked me to stop down the next morning when they were rehearsing for the next show.

"When I showed up, he asked me to stand in the wings and watch the other acts. And that's when you really get an education: being there. And that's how you learn to work in front of an audience. You can study in school all you want, but if you don't try out what you've learned in front of an audience, all of the studying doesn't mean anything. You'll have no way of knowing if they like or dislike you.

"You know, my father wasn't in favor of my going into show business as a way of making a living, so I never dropped out of school. I did all of my performing during vacations. Summers. Christmas. Easter. I could do three shows a day. One matinee, and two evening performances. My sister would sit in the audience and watch me and take notes and tell me afterwards how everything went.

"I didn't want to do only vaudeville. I wanted to be an actress, a legitimate actress who did real plays in a theatre. That's why I had training in the classics.

"An agent by the name of William Menzel helped me get a job with a 10-20-30 melodrama rep group. It was headed by an actress named Laura Hudson. I appeared in *Three Weeks*, written by Elinor Glyn, and I also did a play called *The Devil*. I was a French maid in *Three Weeks*, and I was a tart in *The Devil*. I was about thirteen when I did those roles."

She stops speaking. Someone wants her to sing. She shrugs it off, but when a small group begins to applaud, she girlishly smiles and says, "Well, maybe just one…"

At the end of her second song, she turns to me, and then gestures, "Now, thank the piano player."

As the guests begin to take their cake and coffee, Blllie continues, "The big show that really made people aware of me was Victor Herbert's *Babes in Toyland*. The girl who was playing Jane couldn't finish the run in San Francisco, and the show had four weeks to play in Los Angeles. Even with experience in dramatic and vaudeville, I was apprehensive."

At the end of the run, Billie was without a job. Rather than return to San Francisco, she goes to Santa Monica, a beach community that has been developing into a major resort area. She lands a few jobs singing in cafes along the pier before heading back to Los Angeles.

"I had a job singing in Brink's where a lot of picture people would go. One night the owner introduced me to an agent named George Melford."

When Melford meets Billie, he is scouting new talent for Kalem Pictures, a studio which began operations in Santa Monica in 1908, and is now establishing larger quarters in Glendale.

"When I went to work at the Bristol Cafe," Billie continues, "Mr. Melford would stop in and watch me, and give me suggestions about movement: to stand in one place and sing without any excess mannerisms. My name at this time wasn't Billie. It was Levita, the name I was born with. The Billie came later.

"One of the songs I included in my act was 'Billie' and it went over so well, the newspapers printed my picture with the caption 'Billie' Rhodes underneath. So I kept the name. I used to sing pretty things like 'Meet Me Tonight in Dreamland' and lots of songs about moons, but 'Billie' was always the audiences' favorite.

"Anyway, one night Mr. Melford tells me that Kalem would like to use me in some little girl roles in a few movies. One of their staff people Jimmy Horne, had just completed writing six scenarios and there were parts for a young girl.

"The Kalem studios used a lot of natural sunlight in their movies," says Billie. "Their sets had no ceilings and if they had to shoot the inside of a living room for a domestic scene or society party, they would readjust the canvas covers they stretched over rollers. That was the way they were able to control the light, or indicate the passage of time without having to waste a title like *Later that evening...*

"We acted on platform stages, and, *yes*, we *did* have scripts. That is, we knew what the story was about, and what the intention of each scene was. And we knew where we were supposed to stand or walk.

"We made pictures pretty quickly. A reel a week, and sometimes more. We used local people for crowd scenes, and that made the films seem more natural. A three—reeler took a month to film, and that was considered a feature.

"They filmed stories about everything, even Indian life. They had an authentic Indian star, Mona Darkfeather, who both acted and served as technical adviser.

"It was a nice company, but nobody stayed there very long. That was always the nature of this business. You meet, you work together, and then you go your separate ways. Maybe you meet again. Most times not.

"My leading men at Kalem were Carlyle Blackwell and Paul Hurst. Mr. Blackwell was a handsome leading man. Dashing and rugged, if you know what I mean. We made *Perils of the Sea* together.

"Paul Hurst went on to direct quite a lot of Westerns, and both men went on to talkies. A lot of people think that silent film careers were killed when sound came in, but they don't realize that a lot of those careers might have been finished, sound or no sound.

"I never gave a thought to sound. By the time sound came in, I was singing in nightclubs in Chicago. When that work was over, I went back to singing in cafes in Santa Monica and Los Angeles. I knew very early that when one job is over you have to look for work. If you play your cards right, you can go from one job to another. Not all work is work, but it is work. And not *everything* is quality work. Some jobs are there just in time to pay the rent.

"I was singing in Los Angeles at a cafe where a lot of motion picture people congregated at the end of the day, and I was approached by Mr. Melford who told me that Al Christie was forming a second company at this new studio called Nestor, which would turn out comedies.

"Mr. Christie was a nice man. He had a very good approach to comedy. By that I mean he wanted comedy to grow out of the situation. He didn't like a string of sight gags that did nothing for the story. He used to tell the actor, '*Act! Act!* Don't stand there making funny faces. *Act!*' He hated slapstick comedy. He thought slapstick was vulgar and crude.

"Mr. Christie didn't want to be a Sennett imitator, and turn out an imitation Sennett product. He didn't think the Sennett comedies were all that funny. The people at Sennett's place always seemed to be throwing pies at each other or chasing each other up and down hills, or just playing in mud. Mr. Christie didn't want a troupe of actors to play in mud. He wanted a more refined comedy.

"It was a nice company to work with: Lee Moran, Jay Belasco, Eddie Lyons, Victoria Forde. We were a little rep company. Mr. Christie thought of us as an ensemble and we knew how to play off each other when the cameras were rolling.

"I discovered that I could get better results if I learned how to relax the lower part of my jaw. When you relax your jaw, it lessens the tension in your face. I used to watch Mary Pickford, and I learned not to drop my eyes. A lot of picture actresses used to drop their eyes to be a coquette-type."

"Was Mary Pickford your heroine?" I ask.

Billie nods. "I always admired what she did. She invented what you call silent film acting. She was a wonderful ingenue, better than Lillian [Gish], who was also wonderful, but in the history of this business, it was Mary who was on the screen *first*.

"Mary was a wonderful ingenue, and all of us who were playing ingenues tried to learn from what she did. She had a great economy of movement. Everything Mary did was natural. She knew how to use her face to great advantage. With a camera being right on top of you recording every moment, I learned that by mastering control of my facial muscles I could change emotions very easily. But it has to be subtle and not exaggerated. You're in trouble if you're *caught* doing it. Film acting involves the face more than stage acting. In film acting the camera is right on top of you.

"Of course the kind of comedy I did was light comedy, not the knockabout comedy that Sennett did. His people always had to overreact to get the laugh. Our laughs came from the story. We played characters who had to react to a problem."

"Did you have specific schedules you had to follow?" I ask.

"All of the studios worked on a reel a week principle. We had a lot of theatre to be filled."

Checking the *Universal Weekly* for the weeks of April 10 and April 24, 1915, I came upon the following release schedule for Nestor films starring Billie Rhodes: April 13: *A Mixed-Up Elopement* (Harry Rattenbury, Neal Burns); April 16: *All in the Same Boat* (Jack Dillon, Harry Rattenbury, Stella Adams, Neal Burns); April 27: *His Nobs, the Duke* (Lee Moran, Harry Rattenbury, Stella Adams); April 30: *Her Friend, the Milkman* (Eddie Lyons, Harry Rattenbury, Stella Adams); May 2: *Almost a King* (Lee Moran, Stella Adams, Jack Dillon, Victoria Forde).

When I mention all of these titles to Billie the following year at the Masquers, a theatrical club nestled in the shadows of Thomas Meighan's Los Angeles home, she laughs. "All of those films, if they were done today, would be television situation comedies. They were shot against one or two backgrounds: an *interior*, which would be a kitchen or living room, and an *exterior* which, could be the street in front of one of the character's houses, and possibly the beach.

"I always played the young girl, the heroine, the ingenue. Stella Adams was an older woman. Jack Dillon was the hero-type. We would take our direction from Mr. Christie as we walked through the motions. He would give us our blocking for the cameraman. Then we'd shoot."

"How many cameras did you have on the set?" I ask.

"We had a three-camera set. And we had music to put us in the right frame of mind. That would have been a nice job for you, Stuart, playing all of those moods. A lot of us had favorite songs which would make us feel romantic or sad, or just put us in the mood. Mr. Christie would sometimes give us directions during the actual shooting of the scene. We learned not to look when he gave us direction while he was shooting a scene. We saved film that way, and film was expensive.

"It wasn't distracting, if you could remain in character and keep your concentration. Keep your character moving. Remember: Mr. Christie wanted a relaxed, easy kind of comedy, not of the rough-and-tumble Sennett school."

I ask, "When were the titles inserted?"

"We never knew anything about the titles until after the film was completed. Many times the words we said during the filming became the title. And titles were sparingly used. Mr. Christie liked to have as much actual picture as possible."

"How did you acquire the name, the Nestor girl?" I ask.

"I made my debut in 1914 when Nestor studios were very new. The second company headed by Mr. Christie liked my face, and the way I performed. Other studios also had *girls*: the Biograph girl, etc. So I was the Nestor girl."

To help make the show more successful at neighborhood theatres, the studio sends each theatre, a few weeks prior to the showing, a suitable list of musical selections which could be played during the film by the pianist or organist or little orchestra. Most of the selections are standard music that would be part of any library, but if they don't own these songs, a list of publishers is included where they can be purchased. The audiences of that time used to recognize the selections of the day: "Whispering," "Tango of Roses," "The Merry Widow Waltz," "Glow-Worm," etc.

"Mr. Christie used to poke gently at the foibles of society people," Billie continues. "He liked to show the contrast between the wealthy and the not-so-wealthy. It made for a natural story because of the built-in conflict, which is necessary for all good storytelling.

"The audiences were mostly made up of not-so-wealthy people, who saw motion pictures instead of theatrical plays. If the society people in the film had the same problems as the audience, the audience always felt that they might find the same thing happening to them. Don't forget a lot of people went to the movies to escape and dream. People took movies very seriously, even if they were escapist comedies."

"Billie," I start to formulate my question carefully, "when you have to play for a string of Christie comedies, or Chaplin comedies, in the course of an afternoon or evening, there's a certain sameness…"

"Stuart, you're not seeing these films the way they were meant to be seen. They were meant to be seen one a week, not four or five in the same afternoon. If you see anybody's films in one afternoon at the rate of four or five, you're going to come away with the same feeling: Lloyd, Langdon, Keaton, anybody.

"After a while, all of these scripts become a routine, a product off an assembly line. So did the *Lucy* [Lucille Ball] show on television. When we made those Christie comedies, we were an infant industry. Mr. Christie had developed his own unit, and he had directors working under him, but nothing he did was totally appreciated by the head office. When Mr. Christie began to fight about money, he left the organization.

"I left with Mr. Christie. It was around 1916. Other Nestor people left. Mr. Christie wanted to start his own studio, work with people he had developed, and continue to turn out the type of comedy he believed people wanted to see.

"I had a 52-picture contract. Fifty-two pictures a year. A reel a week. I was signed at $250 a week.

"Mr. Christie wasn't a very good businessman once he had his own place to run. He found himself in bad financial trouble, and a lot of his people soon found themselves out of work. I managed to get my salary, and I stayed around, but when it was time to renew the contract, I told him I wanted to leave.

"Of course, his ego was hurt. He liked me, and he wanted me to stay, but there wasn't anything happening. I had stage offers, and cafe offers, and I wanted to see my family."

Billie never mentions the specific causes of Christie's woes. "I never minded anyone else's business. I did my work, and I went home at the end of the day's shooting.

"Then I rejoined the studio when Mr. Christie had capital to work with. He was going to release his films through the Mutual Corporation. I was in their first Strand comedy, *Her Hero*. I also made *Beware of Blondes* with Cullen Landis as my co-star, and I also did several films with Jay Belasco. They were a lot of fun to make. They were popular, and I received a lot of fan mail.

"But things got a little tough. When I rejoined Mr. Christie and had started making more films, I met Billy Parsons who wanted me to do two comedies for his company, National Film Company. I would do these films on approval, which means I wouldn't get a contract unless the New York office liked them. So, for a while, I had a busy schedule: working for Mr. Christie, and then doubling and doing two films for National Film Company.

"Mr. Christie heard what I had done, and he was quite upset. He'd yell and make all kinds of threats. 'I found you, and I developed your character, and your style of acting and your personality, and now you're going to walk out on me,' and you can imagine the rest...

"Well, The New York office liked the two films I did, and they were going to sign me up at a good salary. Much better than anything I could have made with Mr. Christie. And then they seemed more reliable than Mr. Christie.

"Mr. Christie was always making salary adjustments: half salary, then no salary, then back to full salary when things looked like they were going to get better. He was a very nice man, but you can't just keep people dangling for all their careers.

"So I took this solid offer from Mr. Parsons, which was $300 a week for the first year, $500 for the second year, and $750 for the third year. It was a three-year contract, I did six six-reel features. They were quite elaborate, and they were distributed as Capitol Films by Samuel Goldwyn.

"Louis Chaudet directed one of them: *Hoopla*, a circus story, and he also directed *The Blue Bonnet*. We shot both films in New York City. *The Blue Bonnet* was a Salvation Army story, and they made the clothes I wore in the film, Billy Parsons and I appeared in several two-reel comedies. He was very popular, and he was very well-liked. And I *married* Billy Parsons!"

"You want to know why some people never got ahead in this business?" Billie says in answer to my question regarding talent and breaks. "It was because they kept doing the same thing until audiences were tired of it. You have to keep studying, and keep changing your style, or modifying it, if that is what is necessary. Don't use the same visual jokes in every film you make.

"Mack Sennett, who made a lot of one- and two-reelers in the early days, couldn't make adjustments. His audiences outgrew his type of slapstick humor as *they* matured.

"A wise producer listens to his audiences, and knows how to gauge their reactions. No two audiences are alike, but he should know what goes, and what doesn't go. As people became accustomed to the continuing presence of the motion picture in their life, they kept attending them, and they became very discerning. They grew. They wanted to see *features*. Short subjects were strictly program openers.

"I made twelve two-reelers with Joe Rock for the Grand Asher Distributing Company. They had the place that Columbia has today. Those two-reelers did okay, but they didn't do as well as we had anticipated. I realized I *had* to make a transition to features, if I wanted to last. And if I made a feature, that was no guarantee audiences would accept my humor over a longer period of time. Luckily I made *The Blue Bonnet* and *Hoopla*.

"Some comedians knew they couldn't hold an audience's attention for a six-reel feature. When you look at a two-reeler you know a lot of the story is condensed. Sometimes there isn't much of a story at all, just a lot of action and physical humor. And that's funny, if you are a physical performer. But in a six-reel feature you can't just run around and throw pies to get laughs. You have to have a good, solid story that audiences will accept. Audiences of the twenties were more sophisticated than audiences of the previous generation."

I show Billie the American Film Institute's listings for her feature films she made between 1921 and 1930. There are four entries. 1921: *His Pajama Girl* and *The Star Reporter*. 1924: *The Fires of Youth* and *Leave It To Gerry*.

"I did a lot of independent films in those days," Billie remembers. "Independent films didn't get the same distribution, and you needed a studio behind you to have any decent returns. *His Pajama Girl* was a one-picture deal. At least, that was the way it turned out. I did the film for C.B. Price, an independent distributor. I don't know how the film did. I never saw anything more than some of the rushes. Maybe I didn't care about it when I was told no advance bookings were coming. The company fell apart after we completed it."

I could see she is uncomfortable. Events from four decades ago are suddenly being revived, and discussed. It is simply a matter of talking about the early career of a silent film star who was once the symbol of a studio. This is not a McCarthy Hearing.

I begin again, "Do you have any recollection of *The Fires of Youth*? According to the American Film Institute, there is no available information."

"I came in after they started making the picture. A middle-aged couple starred in the film, and I played their daughter. They never had any real shooting script, and as filming progressed, my part got bigger.

"I left after my work was done, and they were still shooting. I'm surprised the American Film Institute even lists it."

"Do you know what the film is about?" I ask.

"No."

"Did ever see the film?"

"No."

"Any part of it?"

"No."

"What about some of the rushes?"

"No."

"Was the film ever released?"

"I don't know."

I can see Billie is uncomfortable. The talking in the living room has become quiet. The visitors are listening.

I have to continue.

I draw complete silence in answer to my next questions: Who directed the film? Who worked in it? What was the set like?

I repeat an earlier question: Was the film ever released?

"No."

There is no way to end this interview humorously.

"I have a release date of March 28,1924."

"I never saw the film."

"Do you remember the distributor's name? I think it was Ed..."

"I don't know anyone named Ed. Why are you asking about *The Fires of Youth*?

"Because *you* are the only person who could fill in the gaps."

Billie is silent. She shrugs her shoulders. "You know, I worked for six different studios at that time. Some were independent companies who never finished the film. I even got paid for work I never did. It was the easiest money I ever earned, but it tied me up, and I couldn't take any job while I was getting paid for not working."

"What happened to those studios?"

"They had bad financial advisors, or there wasn't enough money. Making a movie is a very unpredictable thing. Maybe that was why I was never really at home in pictures. I was a stage person, and a nightclub person, and there was always another show to do, or restaurant or nightclub to play. They made movies in Hollywood and New York, but there were restaurants and nightclubs, and legitimate theatres, and vaudeville houses all over the country!

"My sister was living in Chicago, and I went there in 1926 to spend some time with her, frankly, just to get out of Hollywood. I think the truth of it was I wanted a change. It was time for a change. Things weren't going all that well, and I thought it may been time to get out, and go for a complete change."

"What was Chicago really like in the twenties? You always hear all kinds of stories..."

She holds her hand up. "Stop! I never worked in a speakeasy, and I never sang at any gangster's private parties."

My visions of gangsters with submachine guns, smoke-filled rooms and Bix Beiderbecke and the Wolverines blasting the Charleston at impossible hours suddenly flew away. I looked at Billie, and I had to laugh. A moment later, we were both laughing.

"And I never sat on Al Capone's lap," she adds. "I know that's what you want to hear, but that was a Warner Bros. view, not totally the truth. I just sang in nightclubs and cabarets. I had new songs, and I changed part of my act when I saw that they were going to extend my engagement.

"One time in Chicago, I think it was 1927, I was singing in some nightclub, and dancing, too, and I was asked to do a movie called *The Gum-Chewers*. Don't look for it. I don't think you'll ever locate it. It was a college production with real college students from the University of Milwaukee. They paid me a good salary, and they paid my railroad fare, and they took care of my hotel bills for a few days' work.

"When I finished my shooting, I went back to the nightclub in Chicago. I had a follow-up engagement in Galveston, Texas for six weeks, I came back to Chicago and did some stage work, and that was it. I stopped working. I simply stopped working."

She stood up. It was getting late. We had been talking for three hours this time. I had several miles to drive to Santa Monica. Some of the guests were leaving while I was assembling the pages of scribbling I had amassed.

Why did everything suddenly stop before 1930? Why hadn't Billie tried to make a transition to sound films? What had she done in the intervening years between 1927, her last recorded date, and the last half-century?

"Make yourself a sandwich," she says, indicating the untouched trays of corned beef, pastrami, roast beef, and ham. "Make two sandwiches. Take one back to the hotel. The restaurants along the beach wouldn't be open this hour. Maybe Zuckey's, but why waste all of this food. There's rye bread, white bread, mustard, mayo. There's still some potato salad left. Go ahead. Eat."

"I'll get you some wax paper. You can't put that on your car seat unprotected. It'll slide all over the place, and you can't eat while you drive on the freeway."

"Billie, why did you suddenly stop working?" I ask after all of the guests have left.

She took a few more steps as if she hadn't heard the question before she turns to face me. The smile isn't on her face anymore, and at that moment, I hated myself. What right did I have to ask someone to suddenly account for the last fifty years of their life?

"Stuart, I was never really that ambitious. I never had any real career drive like a Joan Crawford or a Mary Pickford or a Lillian Gish. Oh, I wanted to work and sustain myself, but I never had *this*." She clenches her hand into a fist. "I never had a *star drive*."

She slowly opens her fist and returns to where I am standing. Outside the street traffic has halted. The porch lights on the adjacent houses have been turned off.

"If a film job was available," she quietly confides to me. "If a stage play was available and I had no other work or chance of work, I'd go after it. Or I'd go and work in a cabaret, or a nightclub. I'd go from one kind of work to another.

"But it's different now. I don't have to do it, and I don't have to prove to myself that I can still do it. I'd do it just to keep myself busy. And that's what I'd tell anyone today. Don't stand still. Be active.

"I was never a wild party girl, and I never lived beyond my means. I saved my money, and one day I just woke up and said, 'I've had it.' And I stopped. I was able to get out gracefully without anybody knowing it, or even missing me!

"Oh sure, I had good times, and it was fun, but it was fun only when I said it was time to get out. And that's exactly what I did!"

"Just like that?" I asked.

"Just like that," she replied. "I wasn't foolish with my money." She stops and looks around the room. "Did I ever mention my *comeback*?"

I reach for my yellow legal pad, but she waves my hands away.

"It's not as dramatic as it sounds. I call it a *comeback*. It was at Los Angeles City College. I wanted to sing with the glee club, and it was many years ago. One of the professors saw my name, and remembered me from pictures, and he asked me to play Amanda in *The Glass Menagerie*.

"I didn't want to do it. I had had a good life. I was married, and I didn't want to get started again. He was very persistent, and Amanda is a great role.

"Big speeches! And some of them a foot long. And I never went up on my lines…And I stayed around to do *The Royal Family*. I didn't plan it. It just happened, and when it was over, I went home and looked after my husband and property."

LABOR DAY WEEKEND: 1980. THE LOS ANGELES.

Film stars and directors are everywhere: Ralph Bellamy, Kathryn Grayson, Eleanor Powell, Sam Jaffe, Gail Sondergaard, Gene Nelson, Rosemary DeCamp, Marian Nixon, and Anita Garvin.

Billie is sitting by herself near the entrance of the banquet room, quietly watching this montage of lobby cards and 8x10 glossies being carried around with the always available felt tipped signature pens. There are shrieks of recognition and constantly popping flashcubes.

"Nice party," she comments when I enter. "But not too many people are here from the old days."

"No, there aren't," I answer. "But you're here."

She shrugs her shoulders. "I guess that's the way it is...Are they going to show any silents tonight?"

Suddenly one of the guests thrusts an 11x14 lobby card in front of her for a signature.

"This is from so long ago," she says. "Where do they find these? I don't think I've ever seen this one."

She smiles as a few people ask her to talk about the stills they have from her films which are being released through Blackhawk, a film company that specializes in films from the silent era.

"You know, Stuart," she says after the momentary rush is over, "here I am many years later and a few years older, and those people talk to me as if I were still a young girl."

She starts to make her way to the front table. Dinner is about to be served.

"You still are young," I say.

She tilts her head and smiles at me. For a moment, the eyes sparkle as if the Kalem camera is on her.

She laughs. "Maybe I am young. Just maybe, but I have nothing in common with that little girl you're going to play for on the screen. That little girl is another person, and that was long, long ago."

June, 1986.

I telephone Billie's niece, Jean Miller, to ask about Billie. What is she doing?

"Billie never stands still," Jean answers. "She sings at a few senior citizens' homes, and has done a few evenings for the Variety Clubs. Other than that, she looks after her property."

Billie has another way of putting it. "When it's nice outside, I'm always doing something. Time doesn't have to stand still all the time. You have to keep busy. That's the most important thing: keeping busy."

■

Billie Rhodes and Stuart Oderman.

Douglas Fairbanks, Jr.

JULY 1968: THE GEARY THEATRE, SAN FRANCISCO.
Ask any early twentieth century theatre-goer. The actor is the role,
and the role is the actor. He creates it, he owns it. It sometimes owns *him*
to the point it won't let him hide his identity in anything else. A lucrative
salary and a constant tour is a blessing and a curse. Ring up the curtain,
and they'll play it.

Joseph Jefferson *is* Rip Van Winkle.

William Gillette *is* Sherlock Holmes.

James O'Neill *is* Edmond Dantes, The Count of Monte Cristo.

Comparisons, when other actors assume roles established by those
who had more than a proprietary interest, are inevitable. How many Ham-
lets can you name?

So it has become with the role of Henry Higgins and his creator Rex
Harrison in *My Fair Lady,* the Lerner and Lowe musicalization of George
Bernard Shaw's *Pygmalion.* Harrison's Higgins is biting and sardonic.
Douglas Fairbanks, Jr., to the delight of the capacity audience, attending
a Saturday matinee performance oozes charm and sophistication in the
manner of a Ronald Colman.

But Douglas Fairbanks, Jr., born December 9,1909, was also in silent
films as well as sound, and is no longer young. That he appeared in over a
dozen silents, beginning in 1916 with an unbilled role in one of his father's
films, *American Aristocracy*, playing a newsboy, is clearly omitted from the
Geary Theatre program.

Walking toward the stage door, I wonder if I should mention that I
had played the piano accompaniment on different occasions for three of

his silents: *Wild Horse Mesa* and *Stella Dallas*, both made in 1925, and *A Women of Affairs*, made in 1928. The leading ladies were Billie Dove, Belle Bennett, and Greta Garbo.

Just moments earlier, an elegant Douglas Fairbanks, Jr., going on sixty years old, had appeared with Liza Doolittle in the Ascot Ball scene, and he, instead of Liza, drew the sighs from the matinee ladies.

Elegance is so obviously a part of the Fairbanks persona, even backstage. While fellow cast members rush about the corridors in tattered bathrobes and sweatshirts and jeans, Mr. Fairbanks, with traces of makeup still on his face, and resplendent in a black and gold smoking jacket and freshly pressed black trousers, receives his folders with his arms folded. He is a portrait of studied casualness, and he observes everything as if he, too, were a backstage visitor who accidentally happened to stumble upon the post-performance bedlam that erupts whenever you are doing two shows a day.

"Something, isn't it?" he asks, gesturing at the stairway to rooms used by the chorus people. "All of that energy. It never ceases to amaze me. In and out, like lightning."

His hair is neatly combed. His offstage voice has a slight British accent, a marked contrast to his Brooklynese delivery in the 1931 Edward G. Robinson gangster hit, *Little Caesar*.

He wishes a good dinner to those who are heading toward a restaurant where advance reservations have been made. He quietly shakes his head when asked if he would like something brought back. What is a "something" for a Douglas Fairbanks, Jr.? Certainly not a pastrami sandwich or a cardboard container of Chinese take-out.

I compliment him on his performance, and how relaxed and at home he appears onstage. Eight performances a week in a very demanding musical, and he makes it look so easy.

He closes his bright blue eyes before he answers. "I never had it easy. Never at any period of my life. I got into motion pictures when I was barely a teenager. Nobody ever opened any doors for me. The Fairbanks name was wonderful for my father, but I was trying to do something to support my mother and myself. Having the same name as my father didn't always guarantee anything. Sometimes it might have been a persuading factor, if someone wanted a favor, to let me put my foot in the door, but I had to do the rest. I had to be able to walk inside, and stay inside! I never had anything handed to me because of my father. I worked all of my life, and I worked hard!

"I started, as you know, with Famous Players/Lasky. I was on loan to Samuel Goldwyn. I worked with Garbo at MGM, but I also worked at studios that were barely surviving. Sometimes we thought we'd never finish shooting, or get our salary!

"Time paints over the hard days, and the rough times, and makes it seem romantic. It isn't! It never was! It was work or no work! I know these young film historians watch *Gunga Din*, *The Corsican Brothers*, and *The Prisoner of Zenda*, and they call these films The Golden Age of Hollywood."

He looks down the now deserted corridor. In the background you could hear the sound of hammering.

"Pure rubbish! There never was a Golden Age! If one existed, I certainly wasn't aware of it, or part of it. And my father was a source of encouragement. My father would say to me, after I started to make some sort of a name for myself, 'You were born with two advantages: height and sound!' Maybe that was his way of proving to me that I had stuck to it, the way he did, and had come through."

Mary MacLaren, who played Queen Anne in Douglas Fairbanks, Sr's, 1921 film, *The Three Musketeers*, explained the strained relationship between the father and the son. "The boy absolutely adored his father, but the father barely acknowledged him. He'd be on the set for days, and the father wouldn't address him by his name. The boy never called him by a parental name: Dad, or Father, or Pop. The father wasn't mean to him, but he wasn't very outgoing, if that's the word for it. The father was a playful boy himself! The son was little more to him than a *tolerated brat*, the way he was treated!"

Screenwriter Anita Loos explained: "The Fairbanks-Mary Pickford marriage was a second marriage for both. She had been married to actor Owen Moore, and both Mary and Doug were huge stars. They were bigger than life. They drew crowds everywhere they went. If you think of the morality of the day, and the attitude toward divorce, the presence of Douglas Fairbanks, *Jr.* may have been a reminder to the father that the boy was a responsibility, and a visible proof that he was getting *older*. Some men don't like or want responsibility when it comes to children, especially children from a previous marriage.

"Mary projected a very wholesome image. She was, you know, 'America's Sweetheart.' She and Doug raised millions of dollars for the war effort. She was very patriotic, and she would have been that way even if she were not in pictures. What was, I think, very sad, was not having children. She wanted children, and to have a family of her own, and seeing that there weren't going to be children, she wanted the father and the son to be close. A parental love instinct, which seems to me to be the most natural instinct to have, after you become a parent, just wasn't there. It wasn't in the father's nature. Junior and Senior were not even *pals*. I've seen fan club presidents treated with more affection and attention. I think the son would have liked to feel an occasional arm around the shoulder and a hug.

"At Mary's insistence, Junior was allowed to write some of the titles in *The Gaucho*. But he didn't get any screen credit. It was conscious attempt on Mary's part to almost make the father realize he had a son, who was about 18, and quite capable of handling adult responsibilities. After all, he had grown up in the business.

"What happened was totally unexpected. By keeping the conversations technical and professional, the son had acquired a technical proficiency that enabled him, years later, to have a successful television career, and film career on both sides of the camera!

"Maybe, because the father was unable to express himself in a loving relationship, he was providing his son with hard-earned experience. Maybe he thought if his son could survive him, he could survive anything.

"But I'm a writer, and writers always try to provide explanations. In real life sometimes there are no explanations. It just *is*, and we have to accept it. I know the son was desperate to be loved by his father. Not just professionally respected.

"Mary eventually divorced Doug, but she always remained close to the son. And the son always remained close to his stepmother. Maybe she thought he would bring his father to his senses, and he would return to her. She never wanted the divorce.

"I remember Mary telling Douglas, the son, after he was signed to play a supporting role to Ronald Colman in *The Prisoner of Zenda*, to ask his father on how he should tackle the role. Now remember this was before the son had made any of the swashbuckler films he would make in the 40's. And the father had made a few swashbuckler films in the 20's that were classics: *The Mark of Zorro, The Black Pirate, The Iron Mask*. Remember, the son was well-established as a leading man, and the father's career was virtually over. He was too old to play either the Ronald Colman lead, or the supporting role that the son was going to do.

"But young Doug, always the dutiful son, and always very respectful of Mary's wishes, asked his father for advice. The father told him, 'Your role is definitely a secondary one, but it's the role I'd want if they'd offer it to me. It's showy. It's actor proof. Anyone could play it, including *you* and Rin-Tin-Tin!'"

Doug, Jr., not content to retire after his film career had diminished, continued to make appearances on talk shows on television, and perform onstage in light drawing-room comedies for which there would always be an audience.

Agent Milton Goldman, commenting on Fairbanks' summer theatre and road tours, told this writer, "Douglas Fairbanks, Jr. will always be a solid bankable performer on the circuit. His name will always mean a sold-out house. He is always cooperative, always approachable. He cooperates with the theatre manager, and the press corps, and members of the audience who want to meet him or pose for a photograph are always happy to discover that he is such a gracious person.

The Pleasure of His Company, which opened on Broadway with Cyril Ritchard, was written by Cornelia Otis Skinner with Douglas Fairbanks, Jr. in mind. And he almost opened on Broadway with it. But, like a lot of actors who have not done theatre very actively, although his *My Fair Lady*, was a big success, *Pleasure* was a *new* play. New plays can be very risky. A new play, an actor who had never done a play in New York: all of these factors ultimately make one turn the role down…in New York.

"George Sanders was like that. He took *South Pacific* on the road after the play was done in New York, and the show had turned a sizable profit. The chance came up to bring the play back to New York, but Sanders was afraid any money made on the road would be lost. He also thought that critics would treat his New York stage debut as little more than something to do until the next film offer came.

"Theatre actors, *real* New York theatre actors, always return to the theatre in New York. They take chances all the time. That is what New York theatre is about: doing an *original* play, doing something new. You fall down, you get up, and try again. You don't retreat to your swimming pool, and fantasize your life away. Every new play is a return to square one.

"Doug did very well with *The Pleasure of His Company* on the road. It was a drawing-room comedy that was specifically tailored to his talents, but I always wished he had opened in New York with it, and then taken it on the road. But the decision was ultimately his, and you have to give him that respect. His tours are always successful, and Doug was always a businessman who knew what was good for business.

"Hans Conreid once told me he was able to have a good career playing the provinces, but he still did a few plays in New York. Confidentially, maybe Doug made the right choice. After so many decades on screen, why should he have to prove himself in New York?

"Cary Grant appeared in quite a few New York plays, but who remembers him as a stage actor? Clark Gable did a few plays in New York, but once he went to Hollywood, he, too, never came back.

"Douglas Fairbanks, Jr. is a link to an era when motion pictures were pure escapism. That he wants to remain active and work on the stage eight times a week is our good fortune!"

■

Douglas Fairbanks, Jr. and Stuart Oderman.

Leatrice Joy

1970: NEW YORK: THE METROPOLITAN MUSEUM OF ART

Leatrice Joy loves to laugh. The capacity audience at the Metropolitan Museum of Art sits in awe as spectacular effect after spectacular effect unfolds on the large screen during a rare showing of Cecil B. DeMille's 1923 classic, *The Ten Commandments*. Leatrice Joy, the star of the film, sits near the piano. She can easily lean across the few feet that separate us and whisper comments and tell me what to anticipate, should that problem ever occur. She is calm and relaxed. I am not. I have never seen the film, and to play it for the first time cold in front of hundreds of people can be nerve-wracking, especially when the original star sits in such close proximity.

I do not have to worry with Leatrice. She is a wonderful audience, and she loves to mumble an occasional "ah, hah," at the end of telling scenes. Theodore Roberts, who plays Moses, always gets a nod of approval. Leatrice sometimes giggles alone at her screen-self. She is wistful whenever Richard Dix appears.

At an appropriate moment, when there is a lull in the action and there are no more chariots or plagues to be presented, Leatrice whispers, "Richard Dix and my friend, Lois Wilson - she co-starred with me in *Manslaughter* for Mr. DeMille - were an item. They made a few films together like *Icebound* and *The Vanishing American*, and they were a successful team, but they never married, even though they were quite fond of each other. I think it was the drinking that ruined them. They were never drunk at the same time. In Hollywood, everything is timing."

Thousands of extras swelter on the beach waiting for the signal to cross the Red Sea. Leatrice, watching the screen, suppresses a laugh as she leans over to whisper. "When the lights come up, pay attention to what I say."

She remains silent for the rest of the film.

When the lights come up, Leatrice rises, stops at the piano to grab my hand to direct me onto the stage for a bow with her as the applause increases. She is easily in her late-seventies with every silver hair neatly in place. Her movements are vigorous and youthful, and onstage she stands ramrod straight. At a signal, we bow to each other, and I return to the piano after she pulls me towards her and envelops me in her arms.

"You don't look old enough," she says in a very pronounced New Orleans drawl, "to have seen this movie in 1925, but this old gal is grateful she can watch it with you in 1970." She points to herself. "Wasn't she something?"

The audience laughs and applauds again. She is decades removed from her screen years as a DeMille star, and she will on several occasions as we appear together in Los Angeles, Washington, D.C., and Connecticut over the next 15 years or so, remind herself in front of everyone that all of this adulation, while most appreciated, is somewhat disarming, since most of the films in which she appeared were made close to 50 years ago.

"You know that Mr. DeMille loved to make movies that took you out of your seat and placed you in another time, another world. He was a great showman who believed that the stage was limiting and could only do so much. You couldn't change the scenes very often, and you couldn't provide the same kind of spectacular effects you could get on a large screen. He read his Bible daily, the Old and New Testament, always looking for new material. There were never any copyright problems, because the stories were thousands of years old!

"He had a wonderful formula for avoiding the censors who would never allow abbreviated clothing to be worn in contemporary pictures. All Bible stories took place in hot countries. If a dancing girl wore next to nothing, you knew she was a bad girl, and bad girls were always punished, usually after an orgy scene, where one or two them, in a long shot, made a few extra dollars because they wore nothing.

"Mr. DeMille knew his audiences, so he let his bad girls be bad just a little while longer before they met their end. Mr. DeMille called this, 'Sin, Suffer, and Repent, but let's give the audience a good dose of sin!'"

She pauses to allow the audience to laugh.

"Wasn't that crossing of the Red Sea something? Do you know how those people crossed the Red Sea?"

Leatrice Joy.

She waits for an answer, as if she were teaching a Sunday school class. "I'll tell you," she announces.

"For days before that Red Sea crossing shot, Mr. DeMille flooded a few streets late at night with gallons of water. It didn't photograph, and he knew he couldn't put all of those extras inside a tank because no tank big enough could be built to contain those people. And where would the water go? You can't walk all of those people in ankle-deep or even waist-deep water.

"Yet it said in the Bible that the Red Sea parted, and Mr. DeMille knew if this film were to be respected, there were extra ingredients needed that were crucial to its success.

"Mr. DeMille was about to give up when he was approached by one of the crew members, who said, 'I think we've solved the problem.' The man produced a bowl of Jell-O, and then he thrust a spoon into the Jell—O, and the spoon remained in position. And it quivered!

"Mr. DeMille was flabbergasted! A bowl of Jell-O! Why not build two clear walls about six or seven feet high and put in thousands of gallons of gelatin? Make the path wide enough to accommodate five or six people across and let them rush through a ten- or twelve-foot passage as quickly as they can, and have these huge fans constantly blowing to create the effect of the sea? You have an establishing shot of the sun at the beach, show the quivering Jell-O, and rush these people through?

"You know there are some Bible translations that say, 'And the water jelled...'"

She winks and laughs. "And that's how the Jews were able to escape the armies of the Pharoah: they ran between walls of Jell-O!"

In early-October of the same year, I visit the Sutton Place apartment of silent film actress Aileen Pringle to report on the Metropolitan engagement. At 11 in the morning, the cynicism of this 1924 Elinor Glyn heroine is in high gear, "Who finds it necessary to come out of obscurity to announce to people that he or she is still alive?" Miss Pringle asks.

"Leatrice Joy," I answer.

"Leatrice Joy!" she shouts. "I knew her, and I always felt sorry for her. John Gilbert was a very big star when they were married, but Leatrice eclipsed him and maintained her success. I don't think he could stand it, but he never said a bad word about her. He also never stayed with her for long periods of time. He was a big drinker.

"I think I told you once before that I worked with John Gilbert in *His Hour*, which was another Elinor Glyn product. John Gilbert often came on the set drunk, wearing clothing which clearly indicated he had been out the previous evening and hadn't the common sense to get changed or washed!

"During a grand ballroom scene, which had to be re-shot a few times, John would slip away for a quick sip of champagne and return a little tipsy as the cameras were ready to roll. He had to pick me up and sway to the music and hold a glass of champagne all at the same time. The man positively smelled, and if you could read lips, you could make out what I said to him: 'If you drop me, you son of a bitch, I'll kill you.'

"He used to wander over to my place on Adelaide Drive in Santa Monica. I had this chaise lounge on the side of the front porch, and I never knew who would be there when I stepped outside in the morning. Sometimes Gene Fowler used it whenever he was unable to make it home. Sometimes Matt Moore used it. For both of those men, I would make eggs, and pack them off to Mass.

"John Gilbert was so handsome, and so charming. He couldn't handle his success or manage his affairs with women. He thought he was in love with them because the new, the latest girlfriend of the moment understood him better than the last. It was all drunk talk!

"After the divorce from Leatrice, he took up with Garbo, my tennis partner. Physically, they were a stunning couple. He was very muscular and tall with those dark brooding eyes, and she was quite sensuous looking with a face that Clarence Bull said could be photographed from any angle. It was impossible to ever take a bad picture of Garbo. The camera simply loved her.

"Garbo was warm when she wanted to be, but she could suddenly become the melancholy Swede and just withdraw and be alone. She could only give so much, and then it would be over.

"Poor John never let this affect him outwardly, but anyone could see it was frustrating him. Sometimes he'd come to dinner without her, but I knew not to pry. It would only make him drink more. I also knew on nights when he came and left early and alone, he would find some eager accommodating waitress, only to be visited by her a few months later and be told she needed abortion money. He was so afraid of the possible publicity he never even checked to see if she were lying!

"The studios had girls available who were very attractive and discreet, but we knew who they were. Hollywood was never a private place, and it was virtually impossible to keep anything a secret for very long. Maybe this was why John always went off on his own. We never knew who these girls were, but he paid the price for it…

"One day he came over and announced that he finally convinced Garbo to marry him. He had this extra bedroom built onto his home just for her. When the wedding day arrived, Garbo never showed up. We made all sorts of excuses to leave. John made all sorts of excuses for her, but he was quite embarrassed and distraught. We never spoke about it, then or afterwards.

"Garbo never saw that special bedroom…but *I* did!"

NEW YORK: 1982

On a September morning my telephone rings a few minutes after eight. I recognize the voice on the other end of the wire. The sound is warm, pure New Orleans.

"Beloved darling, is that you?"

"Good morning, Leatrice. How are you?"

"You know, I've been meaning to call you, but can you believe it? I lost your telephone number. And then yesterday, I opened my Bible…and there it was! Isn't that something? Well, dearest, I have something for us. The Marble Collegiate Church in New York, Dr. Norman Vincent Peale's place, would like me to do my *Evening* for them in November. Are you and your wonderful music available?"

There is a steady downpour of rain and a chilling wind on the night of Leatrice's *Evening*. The meeting room in the basement is full of senior citizens who look old enough to have remembered seeing Leatrice when she was under contract to Nola Studios in 1915 before she went to Hollywood to play supporting roles for the next three years in films starring Doris Kenyon and Carmel Myers. This audience is well behaved, quite the opposite of the jaded film buffs we have encountered during *Evenings* in Washington, D.C. and Los Angeles who come to see the film and debate about print quality.

Leatrice sits at a wooden table which has been pushed against a wall in a small room adjacent to the meeting room. There is a large mirror on the wall. Bright lights on each side accent her still fabulous cheekbones and soulful brown eyes.

I sit next to her and watch her methodically apply her makeup, recalling the words she used to describe the first time she and John Gilbert met in 1918 on the set of *Wedlock* 64 years ago: "We devastated each other!"

In her slip she leans across the table and looks even closer at the mirror as if she wants to seize the image staring back at her.

"You don't mind me like this, do you? I'm sure you've seen women wearing much less. Do I look all right?" She gestures at the white gown which is neatly draped across the chair.

"You look great," I answer.

"You're saying that just to be kind."

She continues to stare at her reflection in the mirror. In the meeting room you could hear the audience lining up to serve themselves turkey and trimmings from the long tables that are covered with red holiday paper.

Impulsively I lean over and kiss her left shoulder. She blinks in surprise and turns away from the mirror.

"I couldn't help it," I explain. "They always do that in the movies."

"Only in period musicals," she laughs. "Is it crowded out there?"

"Packed."

"Packed," she echoes. "You know that during the war, the Second World War, I used to go to the Army base and bring home a few lonely soldiers for a nice homecooked dinner. I couldn't always guarantee the success of the entree but I always served a wonderful dessert...How was *Flesh and the Devil?*"

"Full house," I answer.

"I've never seen it, and I don't want to. Ever."

She rises and pushes the wooden chair away from the table. The conversation has stopped. She heads toward her gown. It is almost show time.

"You know, Stuart," she begins after she has dressed herself, "for some reason there are people who think my marriage to John ended because of Miss Garbo. That's not true. It was never true. During the years John and I were married, Miss Garbo's name was never mentioned. Miss Garbo and I never met, and to this day I hold no ill feelings toward her. John wanted to be free, and as much as I didn't like it or want it, there was no reason to try and stop him once his mind was made up. There was nothing to win. I had to let go.

"John Gilbert was a dear, dear man, but he was very complex. He had problems that he kept to himself, and these problems led to other problems. His mother and father were stage actors who were always touring, always on the road, rarely at home with him. Sometimes the family had times together, most times not. They didn't have a very good marriage. Different temperaments aggravated by the life itself.

"John used to shock Mr. Mayer, who was quite fond of his own mother, by saying *his* [John's] mother abandoned him and that she was a whore, and when he was desperately hungry and there was no food around, he would look in the garbage cans for something to eat."

If she has told this story to others over the years, her eyes betray her. A tear has formed, which she has wiped away with a handkerchief, saying as she quietly laughs, "Look at that! I'm still a Sarah Bernhardt.

"I'll tell you something I've never told anyone before. John once came to my house to visit us. We were living in California, and little Leatrice must have been two or three, and she hadn't seen her Daddy very often. This, I determined, was going to be a friendly visit for her sake. A daughter, after all, should see her father and be with him once in a while.

"While we were at the pool chatting, little Leatrice grabbed her father's watch-chain to listen to the ticking. It looked like an expensive watch, and I warned her to be careful with it. I didn't know where it came from. I thought John bought it. He was always a handsome dresser, and he certainly had an eye for style.

"John laughed and said, 'Oh, let her play with it.' He removed it, and placed it in her hands. 'It's a gift anyway.'

"I was surprised. 'A gift? From whom?'

"'From Garbo, naturally.'

"When my daughter accidentally dropped the watch, I accidentally stepped on it!

"I think, despite all of his successes like *The Merry Widow* and *The Big Parade*, John was afraid that all of his fame and fortune was only temporary, and it wouldn't last forever, and when Metro-Goldwyn-Mayer no longer had any use for him, they would toss him out. John couldn't take or understand the constant demands of his popularity. He was a victim of his success, and a bigger victim of himself!

"But I still love him after all these years. We had some good times together. He could recite poetry beautifully. He gave me a wonderful daughter, and I have wonderful grandchildren, and it is for those reasons that I keep his name.

"I am Leatrice Joy Gilbert!"

Show time!

It is the same evening we have performed in other cities. As the lights dim, I play a chorus of the waltz from Hazel Dawn's Broadway success, *The Pink Lady*, and Leatrice makes her entrance from the wings. In total darkness.

When the lights come up, she stands regally before an appreciative audience that greets her with cheers and bravos. In her white sequined gown designed by Adrian for her Palace Theatre engagement in 1921, the decades have melted away. As she takes a bow, you couldn't help but notice the slit up the side of the dress that shows a great leg.

Connecticut: 1980.

Leatrice performs her *Evening* before an appreciative audience. On this occasion, her performance is in celebration of her 90th birthday.

Her *90th*?

"I added three years onto my age to make people think, 'Doesn't she look wonderful?'"

At the post-performance party at her daughter's home she continues to hold court, sitting in a high backed chair next to a fireplace. On the piano is a photograph of John Gilbert.

Leatrice is wearing the same dress she wore when she performed a few years ago in New York. When I compliment her, she answers, "I'm going to wear it as long as I can wear it. I have the figure for it."

She flashes her leg, winks, and in a purposely exaggerated New Orleans drawl exclaims, "Isn't she a *temptress?*" to a crowd of single and married men of all ages surrounding her.

Temptress or no, she has every man's attention, and she is going to play to them.

A young man, a *Frenchman* of 20, described by my wife as "drop dead gorgeous," stands directly in front of her.

"And who is this handsome young man I see before me? Where are you from?"

"Paris," he answers.

Leatrice rises and advances toward him, "Paris? You deserve a kiss!"

She kisses him.

"And why are you here?"

"I'm a student."

"Ooh! A student! That deserves another kiss!"

She kisses him again.

"And what are you going to be?" she asks.

"A doctor," he answers.

By now everyone was watching.

"Ooh! A doctor! A *French* doctor!"

She kisses him a third time. He was now completely under her spell.

As the guests sample the buffet, Leatrice signs 8x10 portrait stills and scenes and posters from her films, careful to correctly spell the name of each person to whom it is inscribed.

One of the pictures makes her stop to look at it for a few seconds more than usual.

"I haven't seen this one in centuries." She holds up a portrait of a young Leatrice that is visually striking in the way the Marilyn Monroe calendar attracted attention in the 1950's.

"This is dress I wore that was designed by Adrian, but he dyed it to match the suntan I acquired in Mexico. You can't tell where the dress ends and Leatrice begins! I wore it to a nightclub and nearly caused a riot!"

The young French student takes the photo and stares at it.

"Fifty thousand Frenchmen can't be wrong, darling," she says. "But for *me*, you can be *right!*"

She takes his hand as a few cameras record the moment.

"Isn't she the home wrecker?" she asks, waving the picture. "This young French boy will never be the same…Nor will I! Thank you, everybody, for coming to my party at my wonderful daughter's home to be with my handsome grandsons. You can see those John Gilbert genes. Those girls better beware!"

Leatrice Joy loves to laugh.

NEW YORK: 1982.

On March 8, Leatrice Joy appears on the ABC-TV spectacular *Night of 100 Stars*, throwing kisses to a wildly applauding audience who had come to see the best of Broadway and Hollywood together on one stage.

"I've never seen anything like it," Leatrice says a few days later in a telephone conversation. "Backstage it was like a big party! Dressing rooms were crowded with people, sometimes three and four to a room, as if we were young chorus people just starting out!

"Do you know what we did? We brought our cameras, and took pictures of each other! You would have thought *we* were the fans!"

"What's your secret?" I ask.

"No secret," she answers. "A day is a miracle created by God. Go forward and be worthy of it!"

Lois Wilson, Stuart Oderman, Leatrice Joy.

Minta Durfee Arbuckle

1969: SANTA MONICA

In the summer I have a room in July at the Holiday Inn, an area described by people in Los Angeles as "down at the beach," although the Pacific Coast Highway seems to run the full-length of Southern California. In the morning, the area is drenched with fog and the sun never makes an appearance before high noon, and then you realize the ocean really is blue and all beach towels look alike.

After an hour of driving, the homes along Sunset Boulevard into old Los Angeles seem to follow a pattern of architectural regression. The swimming pools slowly disappear, the cars parked in the driveway are no longer new models, and sprawling Spanish-type houses become tiny lawns that never seem green enough to tango upon.

You have to drive very carefully up Coronado Street. All of the houses are of similar construction and the identifying numbers are hidden by tall hedges. Everywhere wrinkled people sit on porches and stare into the hot sun, watching the passing cars.

Minta Arbuckle lives on the fourteen-hundred block. The lawn is well-kept and the garbage cans have been returned to the garage. The window shades are white and fresh-looking and the house has recently been painted.

The corridor between the living room and backroom den is dark, but Minta knows the way. She has probably taken many visitors to where we are going. Along the walls are signed photos of Mack Swain, Charlie Murray, Louise Fazenda, Teddy Sampson, Alice Davenport, Dot Farley, Ben Turpin, Phyllis Allen, and Mabel Normand, but Minta makes no mention or comment. There is nothing to say. At age eighty-one, she has outlived them all.

She opens the door at the end of the corridor and I am face-to-face with a wall-sized full-length portrait of Minta's husband, Roscoe Arbuckle, and their dog, Luke.

"This is the picture I always talk about," she gestures. "This is Roscoe, the most wonderful man I've ever known."

She takes my hand and we enter the room, a further step into the past. She holds up a cracked glass frame under which is a sepia-toned picture of a well-groomed little boy I assume is a young Roscoe Arbuckle.

"Roscoe was always a little boy to me, a great big baby. That's why I can't believe anything people tell me about him. He wouldn't harm anyone."

"This is quite an area," Minta says, as we head toward the site of the old Sennett studio in Glendale. Her hair remains a bright red, the same dazzling color it must have been when she defied her parents and joined Oliver Morosco's troupe at seventeen as a showgirl. "Sennett used to film us around here. Effie Street. Hyperion. Manazita. Echo Lake Park. Blanche Sweet used to live a few streets away with her grandmother, and Slim Summerville used to have rooms in a hotel across the street from Taix's restaurant. You know why so many of these same houses were used in Sennett's films over and over again? Because Mr. Sennett paid these people very well. If they shot in front of your house, you received ten dollars a day. And if they went around your house, you received twenty—five dollars a day. And if they went inside your house, you received fifty dollars a day, but he wasn't responsible for the condition of the furniture. Ten dollars a day in those days was good money, and twenty-five dollars a day on a steady basis could pay off a mortgage in less than two years.

"Some of the homeowners were hired as street extras. They received a dollar a day, plus a box-lunch...Here we are! This is it!"

We stop in front of a large warehouse. The grass along the driveway is brown with neglect. The few windows on the lower floors are cracked or broken. The sun beats down upon the roof with bright indifference.

"I thought the Chamber of Commerce was going to put up a historical marker..."

She cuts me off. "The Chamber of Commerce did nothing because in California they forget about people who don't keep up with the times." Her tone is no longer bright, and her voice is increasingly bitter. "When you're on top, a lot of people seek you out. But when you become a *nobody*, nobody wants you. Sennett was one of the pioneers when he came

Roscoe and Minta Durfee Arbuckle.

out here. There was nothing but grass and horses." She bites her lip. "But the man didn't keep up, and in this ever-changing industry you have got to be aware of the changes. He thought throwing a pie in a two-reeler instead of a one-reeler was adapting to the changing; style and making progress. People got tired of seeing the same old pies."

Back on Coronado Street, Minta leafs quickly through the opening pages of my copy of Deems Taylor's *Pictorial History of the Movies*. She stops on page 31 to tell me that she is the "cross-eyed and slightly blurred victim" receiving Mabel Normand's pie in *A Misplaced Foot* (1913).

"And here I am again," she says, pointing to an irate young lady grabbing Roscoe's collar in *Fatty's Flirtations* (1913).

Her eyes scan the caption above the picture and she closes the book without further comment. "Fatty's career ended tragically...and headlines did their work."

"The newspapers tried him," she says. "It was all done by the newspapers. They had eight editions a day, all of them vicious, all of them against Roscoe. They promoted bad feelings by printing what they *thought* happened in that hotel room. They didn't have any facts.

"You see people in San Francisco always hated people in Los Angeles. And they particularly hated Hollywood people because we had a better climate, and a thriving industry, and they resented the idea of picture people using their town for vacations or weekend hideaways.

"Roscoe and I had separated, but not legally, because there was nothing on paper. We just began to live apart. Roscoe had put his trust in an agent named Lou Anger, and Anger did his best to divide us by making all of Roscoe's decisions. Roscoe hoped we would eventually get back together and he kept sending me checks through my lawyer, Nathan Burkan, who was handling my finances while I was living in New York.

"Mother and I were vacationing in Edgartown, Massachusetts, when my sister Marie called from Los Angeles to tell us the bad news: Roscoe was accused of murdering Virginia Rappe. I couldn't believe it, you see, because Virginia Rappe had been involved with every man on the Sennett lot right down to the grips. Roscoe was in jail in San Francisco on a rape and murder charge because of a party in his suite at the Hotel St. Francis.

"We packed our bags the same night, and we drove all night to New York City to Mr. Burkan's law offices.

"'You know, everyone is talking about Roscoe and Virginia,' Mr. Burkan said. 'The Press is having a grand old time, and I don't think you ought to go to San Francisco.'

"'I'm Roscoe's wife,' I told him. 'Isn't that a proper reason?'

"'You haven't been his *natural* wife for the last four years. You've been living on the opposite side of the country and maintaining separate residences in Los Angeles,' Burkan said.

"Well, I didn't listen to him talking about my inability to find work or my continuing to accept all of those monthly checks. Roscoe sent them to me just to be kind. I don't think he ever thought we were separated. He just saw it as a long period of work that kept us apart. And I just wanted to go back to Los Angeles.

"We were mobbed by reporters at our apartment. All of the New York papers were there, including a few from New Jersey. Even the men from the wire services were there and everyone seemed to have a camera and a pencil. Do I think my husband was innocent? Was Virginia his secret girlfriend? Why was I in Massachusetts while Roscoe was partying at a hotel? Was it true we weren't living together? The whole thing was ironic. A year ago, nobody seemed interested in me and now I was the center of attention. I kept telling them that Roscoe and I were married in 1908 and that Roscoe was a big overgrown baby who wasn't able to handle his own success.

"There were more reporters at Grand Central Station ready to badger us with questions as we were boarding: Did Roscoe know we were going to be with him? What did I think his first words were going to be? How did Roscoe like sleeping in a cell? I wanted to answer them, but Mr. Burkan told us to remain silent. Something we innocently said could be used against Roscoe, you see.

"The conductor escorted us to a private compartment and we weren't allowed to leave for any reason until the train reached Chicago. We weren't allowed to have lunch in the dining car. People kept knocking on the window of the compartment and hoping we would raise the shade. You see, we were famous, my mother and I, as the wife and mother-in-law of a million dollar a year motion picture star turned rapist and murderer!

"Every few hours the steward would stop by and inquire if we wanted anything: a sandwich, some fresh soup, a little snack, an extra blanket. We had worked out a signal by which we could identify him: three knocks, and a short pause, and then three more knocks.

"When we were outside Gary, Indiana, there was a single knock on the door. Mother rose, ready to open it, but I pointed to her seat. That wasn't the signal! Then three more knocks followed and we opened the door.

"The steward wasn't standing there. A man I had never seen before thrust a telegram into my hands. 'Open it now,' he whispered. Don't go back into your compartment!'

"I opened the envelope and read the short message as the train came to a stop. *You and your mother are to follow this man. Important!*

"'Come with me, please,' he whispered.

"We saw the bulge of the gun in his pocket and he took Mother's arm and pulled her into the hallway and down the steps. I had to follow. We walked across the platform to a waiting car. Our luggage was being loaded into the trunk as the man opened the door.

"'Inside, please,' he said, 'and no noise.'

"The side windows of the car were covered with heavy black shades. He told the driver to start the motor. As we pulled out of the station I told him what he was doing was against the law.

"The man with the gun turned around and aimed the gun at my face. 'Shut up,' he said. 'Just sit still and shut up.'

"I don't know how long we drove or where. It was impossible to look out of the windows, and we couldn't calculate how much time had passed.

"When we could see signs of darkness through the front windows, the car stopped and the man got out. He returned a few minutes later and told the driver that everything was waiting for us.

"We kept traveling on back roads that weren't lit until we stopped at an entrance of a large building. The two men got out of the car, went to the trunk, removed the luggage.

"'Before we get you out,' the gunman said, 'I must have your tickets for San Francisco. You're not going to need them.'

"I certainly wasn't going to argue with him and I could see Mother beginning to lose her composure. Maybe we were going to be abandoned here to die. Maybe the prosecution sent these gangsters to kill us so Roscoe wouldn't have any support.

"'Take the freight elevator,' the gunman said, pointing to the red door. 'There's a suite reserved for you. You're in the Morrison Hotel in Chicago. Don't try to run away. You're going to stay here, and everything you need will be here. You won't need a key, and you won't be able to use a phone, and the area outside your door will be under constant watch.'

"Upstairs there were two other men and an attractive woman waiting for us. They had taken the trouble to see that we were fed, but there was one hitch: the attractive woman took her meals with us. At the end of each meal, she nodded to the two men and they removed the silverware and dishes. She left with them, and we had no further disturbances.

"The next morning, the same ritual was observed for breakfast: two men with a long silver tray, and that same attractive woman. Again, we ate in silence. 'You'll be out of here soon enough,' one of them said. 'You're lucky. They've kept people here for three weeks at a time.'

"Two days later, the attractive woman handed Mother a pair of tickets. 'You're going to leave,' she said, 'but not from Chicago. You'll leave from Oak Park. The Oak Park train will then come *back* to Chicago. Nobody will be watching for the Oak Park train. They'll be watching all of the New York trains coming *into* Chicago.'

"We were more than ready to leave. The two men took us down in the same freight elevator to the same touring car with the same black shades over the side-windows. But another man drove us to Oak Park.

"We rode in silence and when we reached the station, a new man put down his newspaper and walked over to us. 'I'm going to ride with you to Chicago,' he told us. 'Just look very natural and remain calm. And when the train pulls into the Chicago station, I'm going to leave you. The code word is silence.'

"We boarded the train and were hidden in another private compartment. The shades were drawn and the door was locked. The man with the newspaper sat across from us and he read the entire time, never putting his newspaper down.

"Shortly after midnight, there was a series of three knocks, a short pause, then three more knocks. I switched on the light, and opened the door.

"The man with the newspaper quickly stepped between me and the door, looked into the corridor, and disappeared.

"The steward handed us a small tea tray and before I could ask Mother if she wanted anything, the steward stepped out of the compartment.

"Well, drink it,' Mother said. 'They don't give us chance to choose what we want to eat, but I doubt if they are going to poison our tea!'

"I lifted the cup to my lips and then dropped it to the floor. The tiny piece of newspaper that was resting underneath the cup escaped un-soaked.

"Mother reached down for the newspaper. 'I guess the dishwasher...'

"'That was no dishwasher's careless error,' I said. 'Read what is written on the newspaper!'

"Mother held the newspaper to the light. 'Dear Minty,' she read. 'I knew you would come!'

"*Minty*,' I repeated. 'Only Roscoe calls me Minty. Look at the handwriting! It's from Roscoe!'

"Shortly after we arrived in Vallejo, the train stopped. But I didn't hear anyone arriving or departing. A few minutes after we started moving, Mother and I heard the familiar signal at the door.

"'May I speak with you, Mrs. Arbuckle?'

"It was the man who had given me the telegram when the train stopped at Gary, Indiana. I tried to close the door, but he had jammed his foot in its path.

"'I really must speak to you' he repeated.

"'I don't know who you are. I don't care who you are,' I said, 'but if you don't go away and leave us alone, I'm going to scream, and I don't care who hears me!'

"He took a closer step toward me and forced himself inside the compartment. 'I wouldn't do that,' he said. 'You might call attention to yourself and further damage your husband's case.'

"'I'm on my way to my husband right now,' I told him.

"'May I introduce myself?' the man said. 'My name is Milton Cohen and I am Roscoe Arbuckle's attorney. I must spend some time with you. You have no idea what has been happening.' He held up his hand. 'You were not kidnapped. You were rescued. If we didn't take you *they* would have kidnapped you.'

"'Rescued?' I couldn't believe what I was hearing. 'We weren't allowed to read any newspapers or make any telephone calls.'

"'That was all part of the plan,' Milton Cohen said. 'The prosecution in San Francisco wants to make a killing, and Roscoe is the perfect victim. They're watching all of the trains to see if you'll come back to Roscoe. They don't want you to stand by Roscoe. It damages their case if the wife stands by her husband. It takes away from the image they want to put in the newspapers: an overweight comedian is a sexual pervert who took unfair advantage of an inexperienced young girl.'

"'Virginia Rappe is not what any man on the Sennett lot would call inexperienced...'

"'Roscoe's size is against him, Minta.' Milton Cohen said. 'There are rumors going around that Roscoe got her drunk in his suite and when she wouldn't go into one of the rooms with him, he forcibly dragged her and slammed the door and raped her with a Coke bottle!'

"I couldn't believe what I was hearing. *A Coke bottle?*

"Milton Cohen shook his head. 'A rumor, Minta. They didn't find any Coke bottles near her, but one of the bellboys said there was a steady supply of bootleg hooch coming in the entire day.'

"'Mr. Cohen, anybody can get liquor...'

"The attorney shook his head. 'I know they can. And do. But you are not supposed to be *caught* with it in circumstances like Roscoe's. The prosecution wants a scapegoat. The people of San Francisco are tired of people from Hollywood coming to their town and using their town as a weekend playground. Roscoe has a reputation for wild parties and getting drunk and getting into all sorts of fights. And Roscoe is *fat*. *Fat* drunks are *mean* drunks. And since Virginia Rappe died under mysterious circumstances...'

"'And I suppose all of this is Roscoe's fault?'

"'Minta, they're saying Virginia was *crushed* to death. Her bladder was broken because a violent weight was thrust...'

I saw Minta glance across the room at the cracked picture of her husband.

"You know, Stuart," she continues, "I stood by Roscoe through all of the trials. *Three* of them. *Three* trials because the jury couldn't reach a verdict on the first trial. And after the *third* trial, Roscoe was acquitted. The jury deliberated less than two minutes and returned with a verdict of acquittal *and* a formal note of apology.

"The courtroom was absolute bedlam. Everybody cheered us, and Roscoe and I went back to Los Angeles together for the first time in years.

"But it didn't last very long. You know Roscoe was always afraid I would bring up what happened in that hotel suite. He knew that I had heard the rumors, and maybe he thought I believed those rumors were true.

"Even after the divorce, we were still good friends, and his next two wives never minded his visiting me. We would meet for lunch and talk as if nothing happened in that hotel suite. But I knew he was afraid I would get angry at something and bring it up.

"He even talked about marrying me again, but he never asked me formally. He never said anything close to it. Sometimes we'd go for a drive and he'd take my hand and say, 'Wouldn't it be nice *if*...'

"Well, my dear, you can't live together based on *if*. You either do or you don't. And frankly I didn't want to pick up after him a second time, and have to telephone people he offended the night before. I had enough of that side of him."

She looks at the cracked framed picture of Roscoe and half-smiles.

"Roscoe wouldn't have been able to do anything to that girl. Because he couldn't do *anything* most of the time. Maybe that was why those rumors were started. Because Roscoe couldn't do *anything*.

"And maybe she *laughed* at him…"

It has grown darker outside, and the neighborhood has become strangely quiet. Minta reaches across the night table and switches on a small lamp. The light casts eerie shadows on the worn drapes and faded paint on the walls. She is a survivor, and when one is the *last* survivor, the *final* survivor from the Sennett lot, one must be incredibly lonely.

"I can laugh at those pictures on the walls," she says, "but no matter how hard or how much I laugh, those pictures don't laugh back."

She walks over to the cracked framed picture of her husband and touches it gently. "Roscoe was always a little boy to me, a great big baby. That's why I can't believe anything people tell me about him. He wouldn't harm anyone, and I still love him…"

■

Stuart Oderman and Minta Durfee Arbuckle.

Aileen Pringle

NOVEMBER 1968: NEW YORK CITY.

Silent film star Aileen Pringle's East 57th Street apartment is incredibly small, but is large enough for her, as she makes full use of every available space with bookcases of all sizes. Where there are no books there are end tables. And on the end table there are books, but those books have not been read. They are loans from friends, who realize they wait to have them returned, but they will be returned, and they certainly will have been read.

Both walls of the corridor leading to the book-crammed living room that looks down on an always busy East 57th Street are crowded with signed photographs of Valentino, Marion Davies, Rachmaninoff, and George Gershwin.

Without any provocation, just a lingering stare from an interested visitor, she will say a few words about each person whose photograph has caught your interest, even if only temporary.

Valentino: "I was his date for the premiere in New York of *The Son of the Sheik*, probably his most successful film, and fortunately his last. *Un*fortunately, his type, the dashing virile lover who lures repressed English woman *in* or *out* of tents was becoming a *cliché* which was beginning to be a subject of low comedians' nightclub humor. With the coming advent of sound, Rudy had more than enough of a good reason to be concerned. His accent was very thick, not hard to understand, but it didn't fall as easily on the American ear as a *French* accent. Charles Boyer was just around the corner, and while both men were the object of women's fantasies, I think Boyer wasn't so exotic and remote."

Marion Davies: "A spoiled Ziegfeld girl who was raised by her mother to be a rich man's *dolly*, and not to settle for anything less. A *wonderful* natural comedienne. When she became involved with the newspaper tycoon William Randolph Hearst, who was very much married, her strict Irish brand of Catholicism forbade her from ever thinking of marrying a divorced man, no matter who or how wealthy he was. Hearst wanted to make her a serious actress, because he felt, being so much older, and sort of grand-old-walrus-type, that when you laughed at Marion you were laughing at him. But I will say one thing about Marion's loyalty: when the Hearst papers could have gone under, it was Marion whose money saved the day. Say what you want about her. She was very, very loyal."

Rachmaninoff: "He lived right around the corner from my bungalow in Santa Monica. A wonderful pianist, a great wit, and an excellent bridge player. Santa Monica has evolved into a little European colony of people who weren't going to fall the phony Hollywood lifestyle which existed even back them. Think of it, within a few miles of Adelaide Drive: Aldous Huxley, Sergei Rachmaninoff, Igor Stravinsky, Christopher Isherwood!"

Gershwin: "George?" she laughs and goes to her bureau, returning a few moments later with: a few unbound sheets covered by two faded brown leatherette covers on either side.

She gently places the semblance of a scrapbook on my lap.

I open to the first pages, and see a parade of what amounts to little more than a passing parade of stick figures primitively drawn or sketched India ink scenes with a one- or two-line caption. Some of the figures address each other with dialogue framed by comic book clouds.

"What do you think?" she asks, her eyes close to mine, and I am instantly thinking of the situations in *Three Weeks* and *His Hour*, novels written by Elinor Glyn, whose heroines lounged on bearskin or tiger skin rugs, the more conducive to seducing unworldly or very experienced European travelers. "Unless, you are too baffled…"

"They're okay," I answer, "Whose drawings are they?"

"George Gershwin's!" she beams, "And I can see the expression on your face almost changing. But not enough to be impressed. His paintings were better, but he liked to *doodle*, and that's why I still have them. He put himself through such pressure, hoping to be a Maurice Ravel.

"And when they finally met, Ravel said, 'Why do you want to be a second-rate Ravel, when you are already a first-rate Gershwin!' George wanted to conquer all three worlds: the Broadway of New York, the film world of Hollywood, and the concert-halls of Europe!

"He certainly did those things, but his European reputation, based on his

Aileen Pringle.

opera [*Porgy and Bess*] and the *Concerto* [*Concerto in F*], and, of course, *An American in Paris*, have grown in stature only after his death. In that regard, in composing the last three works, he was shunning the commercialism of Broadway and Hollywood, and trying to courageously enter the arena of the Old World masters. That's quite a long way from Al Jolson singing 'Swanee'!"

On the wall is a yellowing 8x10 glossy of a morning trip to the Los Angeles Union Station with *Gentlemen Prefer Blondes* author Anita Loos on an incoming train also bringing the author of *The Three Black Pennys* and *Java Head*, Joseph Hergesheimer, to the film capitol. Aileen is carrying a huge black domino.

"That man, Hergesheimer, was a much respected author in his day, and he's barely a footnote now," she tells me as I consciously stare at a pencil sketch, *Pringie by George Gershwin: July 26, 1931*, resting on a coffee table covered with copies of *The New Yorker* magazines.

"I've been watching you looking at the walls and bookcases," she says. "You're probably memorizing everything in sight with that mind of yours. Go ahead: pull any book out of the bookcase and see what I have. I know you're dying to do it. You've been sitting there like the Victor Dog waiting to hear His Master's Voice!

"I sent for you because of your letter. I didn't think anybody showed silent films anymore, and I never thought anybody would go to the trouble of learning how to play for them. If you had said you had played for mine, I wouldn't have invited you up here, because L.B. (the B stands for *Bastard*: the man thought the sun would actually rise because he ordered it) Mayer *burned*, actually *burned*, my prints in 1952 before I came to New York. It was a typical Mayer move of that period. What you couldn't sell to television, you destroyed. Who was it that mentioned my name in Los Angeles?"

"Claire Windsor," I answer. "We met at the Masquers…"

"*Claire Windsor!*" she bellows, "You mean *Olga Kronk*, the beauty contest winner who was awarded a Hollywood contract, don't you? You mean she's still alive? I know her career died years ago. I can still remember taking a cross-country train with her from Los Angeles to New York. Do you know what *Miss Kronk* did for the entire duration of the trip? She put on makeup. Isn't that exciting?"

In my lap I am holding a first edition of Theodore Dreiser's *An American Tragedy*, a two-volume boxed set. Later copies, according to Jerry Devine, who played the juvenile in John Barrymore's *Sherlock Holmes*, were large one-volume books which had little value in the collector's market.

"What was Dreiser like?" I ask.

"Theodore Dreiser had very leftist leanings," she answers, "but like a lot of those boys who got a taste of capitalist money, he changed his political tune and he had his accountants going to Horace Liverweight's [his publisher] office to check the weekly sales and grosses to make sure he wasn't being gypped out of one cent!

"One time Dreiser and I were seated next to each other during lunch at the Algonquin. You know that crowd: [Heywood] Broun, Dotty Parker, Edna Ferber, Marc Connelly; and while we were having lunch, I felt this hand resting on my thigh for a little while longer than was the accustomed standard. I said to Dreiser, 'Mr. Dreiser, it is a good thing for the two of us that this tabletop isn't made of glass!'

"Red [Sinclair] Lewis was a most unattractive man with the worst complexion you ever saw. His face, with those red sores, made him look like an unbaked pizza pie. It must have hurt him every time he had to shave, but he had a wonderful eye on the foibles of America. He dedicated *Elmer Gantry* to my friend H.L. Mencken, who was the editor of *The American Mercury*.

"Henry [H.L. Mencken] told me that during the initial uproar over *Elmer Gantry* that Lewis once walked into one of these Holy Roller churches that he was satirizing, and he took out his watch and yelled to the ceiling of the church, 'If God exists, may be strike me dead!' And when nothing happened, he shrugged his shoulders, and walked out.

"I'll tell you an interesting Sinclair Lewis story. One time he and I were seated next to each other for lunch at the Algonquin and I felt this hand resting on my thigh for a little while longer than was the accustomed standard…Would you like to hear a sensational Eugene O'Neill story? One time we were seated next to each other for lunch at the Algonquin…"

The wit is still stinging and she knows it. It is evident in a *Saturday Evening Post* interview on March 20, 1928:

"In the British West Indies (date of birth: July 23, 1895) my life was monopolized by selfish pleasures, a silly round of social bustle, teas, tennis, polo, dancing, house parties, midnight picnics, sessions of baccarat, *vingt-et-un* and suppers with 17 Indian servants who were there to anticipate every wish. If I had stayed there, I would have vegetated to a large purple cabbage. What a fate!"

"How did you manage to escape?" I asked during a later visit.

"A woman's role was very defined in those days," she recalled. "I was fortunate to have parents who provided me with a wonderful education. I went to the Madames of the Sacred Heart [a convent school in Paris], and the McKenzie School of Economics in London. When we were living in San Francisco, the city of my birth, I took piano lessons from a lady who told me she was one of Jack London's girlfriends. *The Call of the Wild*…"

"What was he like?"

"Stuart, I was only a little girl," she laughs, "but I remember he came by on a few afternoons to wait for her. He looked like a waterfront ruffian, but he wrote beautifully. I think he believed that he could only write about rough-and-tumble times if he actually lived them, rather than stand at the sidelines and only observe them. He would get good and drunk and go looking for a punch out, and write about it. I know that a few people in San Francisco told me years later that Jack London went to Alaska during the Gold Rush and that he took a young prostitute with him for company. He must have been about sixteen, but he obviously knew how to handle himself well.

"I had a most unusual sex education. My mother wasn't the most verbal about that sort of thing, but she knew I had to know something about it. So, at the age of twelve, and how she did this I'll never know, she took me to a sporting house on Nob Hill. I found myself dressed in one of flashy gowns those ladies wore, and I was standing alone at the top of the stairs.

"She told me to *slowly* walk down the steps right into the front parlor where she was sitting. Remember: this was back in 1907, a year after the famous earthquake, so I guess my mother figured she has *carte blanche* to walk everywhere, because city streets, in some sections, were still in ruins. The only thing I learned from that experience was to keep my head high and avoid eye contact. It was a look I tried to keep in my MGM days when I played stiff-necked queens standing on balconies proclaiming, 'Do not be disturbed, my people! The war is over!'"

During an afternoon visit in the early Seventies, she recalled, "I turned down a lovely job at *Vanity Fair*, and against the wishes of my mother, my father, and my husband, I made my stage debut in a play called *The Bracelet*. Now remember: this happened in 1915, this act of fighting for what I wanted to do. Women didn't speak up very often in those days, Ibsen's *A Doll's House* or no! Defiance was certainly *not* in order!"

She deliberately pauses to pour herself another cup of tea. I have been eating most of the cookies. I wasn't going to let them go to waste, and she certainly wasn't taking many.

"My family made a me brilliant, if not wonderful, marriage to the son of the former Governor of the Bahamas. Charlie [husband Charles Pringle] later went on to become the Lieutenant Governor of Jamaica, and had we stayed together I know that would have meant more hot days and constantly changing clothes."

Aileen Pringle came to Hollywood after appearing on stage in New York with distinguished actor George Arliss at the Booth Theatre in a production of *The Green Goddess.* "I was an *Ayah*, an Indian servant girl, and I came into the production shortly after it opened."

One of her press interviews serves as a portend of things to come:

"I have come for the money. All I want is fame. High society and movies don't mix well. My career depends on whether I can or cannot act. It hasn't a thing to do with whether my husband is a plumber or a duke!"

"How successful were you in the early days?" I ask.

"I was in a low-budget film shot in Florida called *Stolen Moments* with Rudolph Valentino, who had been in some twenty or so films. He always was able to get film work, but nothing of any career building significance until he was cast the following year [1921] in *The Four Horsemen of the Apocalypse.*

"But *Stolen Moments* never did anything for either of us, but pay our rents. Given the roles we played, you're not missing anything. I *never* met anyone who saw it, and I'm not going to ever bring it up, except to you, because you'll bring it up, and I don't remember it, and it isn't worth talking about.

"I went from film to film, proving to myself that it was possible to get work. That's all any profession is: *work.* Getting *work.*

"The Valentino he became was not the Rudy I knew when we did that film together. He was a struggling actor, and a wonderful dancer. He made *any* partner look good, the way a Fred Astaire could. But they were not the same type of dancer. When Rudy became a major star, he *masked* his personality. He became the *Lover*, and to those of us who knew him, he was always Rudy. Cary Grant was the same way: always charming, always a gentleman. Once when I told Cary that my radio was being repaired, he had his driver send over his Atwater-Kent radio to my home in Santa Monica, which was not ever a flashy area. It was out-of-the-way, and very quiet, a suburban area, especially in those days.

"I had a place in Santa Monica at 722 Adelaide Drive. We were near the beach and far enough away from the movie people, who were little better than your shop girl and the merchant class. You had shop girls like Joan Crawford trying to impersonate society people, and you had real people from society like myself, who had more than an eighth grade education, doing little more than walk-ons…Until *Three Weeks.*

"*Three Weeks* was the *salacious*, forbidden book of the day. They would say call it 'The book you read behind closed doors,' or 'The book you read when everybody was asleep.' Anything to attract an audience. It was written by a silly Englishwoman named Elinor Glyn, the lady whose singular contribution to literature was the word, *It*.

"Fan magazines used *It* to describe Clara Bow, Colleen Moore, girls who danced the Charleston, or drank bootleg liquor, or had loose morals, or came home late at night, and might have a drink or two too many...*It*!

"*Madame* Glyn, as she wished to be addressed, would look at all of the incoming actors and actresses, and if you met with her approval, she would announce, to whoever dumb enough to listen, that you had *It*! Her books made a lot of money for the studios, and the studio people hung onto every word she said. This nonsense could only happen in a place called Hollywood, where fantasy created fantasy.

"People thought I looked like Elinor Glyn, and I became the *Madam's* personal choice to play the Queen of Sardinia, the vamp who seduces a young virginal Englishman [Conrad Nagel] in the most exotic of circumstances. This was a prestige film, but I knew they had wanted me to be another Theda Bara-like vamp, although they tried to group me with Gloria Swanson and Joan Crawford."

I ask, "What was Joan Crawford like? Her daughter presents quite a shocking picture..."

"I worked with Joan in *Dream of Love*, which Fred Niblo directed[1928]. She had very little formal education, but she was always very professional, punctual, easy to work with, and extremely ambitious. If Joan's daughter wanted to ruin her mother's career and reputation with *Mommie Dearest*, she should have done it while Joan was alive.

"If this little girl had as much nerve as her mother, why did she wait until her mother died to write this book? Do you think she would have done this when her mother was alive?

"I doubt it, and she was given everything.

"I'm not defending Joan. Joan was a woman trying to survive on her own terms in a man's world. When the studio let her go at the age of forty, she knew she was finished, and she had no other way of earning a living. And she had her family to support. When Joan went on that television soap opera to substitute for her daughter, she was fighting to maintain her daughter's employment. What could that no-talent daughter have done without her?

"Joan never had it easy. She had managed to marry into the Pickford family via Douglas Fairbanks, but she wasn't able to handle Mary. I knew Mary, and her brother Jack. Jack, if I remember correctly, was always getting girls into trouble, and he had large private parts. Mary certainly wasn't very nice to her. At the time of Joan's entrance into Pickfair, Mary's career was in jeopardy. It was the start of the Jazz Age, and here comes this sensational Charleston dancer whose mother-in-law is only a few years older. How do you think Mary felt? Mary was still playing little girls who romped with farm animals when she was well past the age of puberty!

"I remember when Joan attending one of my dinner parties. Midway during the evening, John Gilbert came over to me and whispered that I should go immediately into the kitchen…There was Joan, talking to the chef, asking him to duplicate the exact same meal he was serving at my house, should she ever have a dinner party at her house!

"Poor Joan! She thought she had to imitate everybody else! Isn't that pathetic to have such a low opinion of yourself? The reason she was so successful in *Mildred Pierce* was very simple: she *was* Mildred Pierce.

"When the costume department was trying to dress her, she took them right to a department store and picked out an actual waitress outfit from the rack in the basement! I think it may have cost six dollars, at the most. Joan took it off the rack and said to, I think it was Adrian, or someone like that, 'This is what Mildred Pierce would wear! I *was* a waitress! I scrubbed floors on my hands and knees! I *am* Mildred Pierce!'

"James M. Cain, the author of *Mildred Pierce* was my second husband. I think we were married for twenty or twenty-five minutes. We had known each other for quite a long time, and we would always run into each other when we were involved with other people. When we were both free in the 1940's, we were married.

"The marriage was a disaster. We were both competitive. That sort of thing doesn't work over any period of time. Unless both people are *working* at the same time. Otherwise the relationship or the arrangement becomes a sort of *what will you be doing when I'm out?*

"Cain was a late success. He was a newspaper man who turned to writing mystery novels when he was over forty. The first was *The Postman Always Rings Twice.*

"Cain always sent me flowers on my birthday until he died. I'm glad to see younger writers reading him with the same respect they show Raymond Chandler. Jim Cain was a fine writer. Read Albert Camus' *The Stranger* right after you finish a Cain mystery. Those opening sentences of *The Stranger* could have been written by Jim Cain.

"Cain had a very realistic attitude about Hollywood. When *Postman* came out as a film, and people would stop him and ask, 'What do you think of what

Hollywood did to your book?' He would answer, 'My book is on the shelf. I just made a little extra change.'

"He was very realistic about Hollywood, about the printed word, and the visual image.

"When the Gershwin brothers, George and Ira, came out here to Holly-wood, George absolutely hated it! He thought he was going to reach bigger audiences with concertos, but the studio chiefs told him they wanted *songs*. He and his brother, Ira, who liked Hollywood, and the Hollywood life, wrote the words and music for the RKO movie *Delicious* for Janet Gaynor and Charles Farrell. George wrote his *Second Rhapsody* at my house in Santa Monica. Those cartoons on the walls and the 'Pringie' pencil sketch are my souvenirs of his stay. He also wrote parts of what became *Porgy and Bess* at my house. He had many spiraled music notebooks, and he would take down a few measures and keep them until an occasion came and he had to use them.

"Notebooks, folded-up blank music sheets: all writers use those things. You're thinking all of the time. Not consciously, but suddenly you get that shock of inspiration, and there is no piano in your immediate vicinity...

"Vincent Youmans saw Hollywood for what it was: a good place for song-writing, and an opportunity to spend some time in the sun. Whenever he came over to visit, and if my mother didn't know he had just arrived, he would announce his presence by playing the first four bars of his 'Tea For Two.' When she died, I shocked the congregation of our church by having the organist play an entire chorus of 'Tea For Two' instead of some traditional stodgy hymn. I told our minister that 'Tea For Two' meant more, so why shouldn't it be played?"

June 1985: The Museum of Modern Art in New York City has scheduled a mini-series of John Gilbert films, including the popular *Flesh and the Devil*, and the rarely shown *Man, Woman, and Sin*, co-starring Jeanne Eagels. An anticipated *His Hour* was not included. It was one of the MGM efforts that Mr. Mayer had allowed to go into ruin.

Aileen recalled, "John Gilbert was one of the saddest men I ever knew. On the set, he was a great charmer and very professional. He was under a lot of pressure and he wasn't able to handle the role of being a popular idol. I know about the lip readers who say I was cursing him in one of the sequences.

"They are right. On the day that sequence was shot, Mr. Gilbert was very drunk, and he was whirling around the ballroom floor with a glass filled with *real* champagne. When he started to get a little too tipsy, he would spit out some of the champagne, and it would fall on my bare shoulder. I know I called him a son-of-a-bitch, but it was deserved. What neither of us knew was that it was the "take" that would finally make it to the big screen.

"I had a diaphanous gown that left nothing to the imagination for one of the scenes and Mr. Mayer came down from his tower to *supervise* the proceedings which involved my reclining on a bear-skin rug. Naturally, Mr. Mayer wanted several "takes." One of his messengers sent a note to my dressing room, stating that Mr. Mayer wanted to see this diaphanous gown in his office at the end of the day.

"I knew what that old goat had in mind, but I didn't want to disappoint him. At the end of the day, I sent the gown to Mr. Mayer's office in a lovely white box with the card whose message announced: 'Dear Mr. Mayer: Here is the gown that you wanted to see. I hope it fits!'

"Because of that, I lost two prestige films to my tennis partner, Greta Garbo: *Anna Karenina*, which was released as *Love* and co-starred John Gilbert, and *The Temptress*. I also rejected *Ben-Hur*, because I didn't want to be subjected to all that heat and chariot dust.

"Mayer was no fool. He knew that Garbo and Gilbert were one of the biggest box-office attractions in the history of films. And John, poor John, was absolutely crazy about her! He even had an extra bedroom added to his house in anticipation of their marriage. When Garbo failed to show up on the wedding day, he was very crushed. Garbo never saw that beautiful bedroom!'

"I know that book about John Gilbert written by his daughter [*Dark Star* by Leatrice Fountain] is a loving tribute to a father she rarely saw, but some of her research comes from movie magazines. If John read any of the classics, he never discussed them with me. The only reading I ever saw him do were the words on a whiskey bottle. John was a very kind man who was always getting into trouble with waitress-types who would call him *months* after they had spent a weekend together. They always said they were pregnant, and John would always quickly give them abortion money, much more than the usual rate because of who he was. And not even bothering to have their claims verified. It was easier to pay them off with more money than they deserved. He knew what would happen to his career if the studio ever found out. He spent many an evening on my chaise lounge in order to avoid being picked up for driving under the influence.

"That chaise lounge supported a lot of men. B.P. Schulberg, a producer at Paramount and father of the writer, Budd, was a terrible insomniac. He was a good dominoes player and lived almost across the street. He spent a few nights at my place. So did the writer Gene Fowler. I cooked breakfast for all of them.

"I guess you had to be able to adapt to the ways on the motion picture industry, if you wanted to be a success. In no other profession would you find yourself working with people that, under normal circumstances, you would never invite to your home. A man can have bad manners and worse morals, but he still could be a fine director."

She breaks into loud laughter when I read aloud a statement she gave to the *Saturday Evening Post* for their issue of March 27, 1927:

"Aileen Pringle, always in pursuit of but never getting the man, frankly described herself: 'I am always back at the house-wrecking job, bringing happy homes to the verge of ruin with neatness and relish. No matter how weak the heroes or heroines of the movies are by the sixth reel, they get a gland attraction for a drink from Ponce De Leon's Fountain of Youth just before the time to end the last reel by living happily ever after.'"

"Even then I was disillusioned with the studio," Aileen Pringle reflected almost six decades later. "When Maurice Tourneur directed me in *The Christian* [1923] there was a scene in a dining room which was totally wrong. I was acting as the hostess of a dinner party, and Tourneur, for the purpose of putting action and movement in the scene, wanted me to stand and remain standing until everyone was served. I told him that if he came from the *proper* background where this type of dinner party was *de rigeur*, he would know how to behave during a party of this sort, and *how* to direct the scene!

"The studio chiefs really didn't know what to do with me, so they made me an unofficial 'greeter' of the New York writers as they stepped off the train. I knew that Mr. Mayer's people were buying properties listed in *The New York Times*, and I also knew they hadn't bothered to read any of them. I always brought books to the day's shooting because I was bored, and I couldn't take all of that time-wasting between 'takes' and 'breaks.' I don't know how many trips I made to that Union Station early in the morning, but I greeted Rupert Hughes, Ernest Boyd, Governeur Korris, Theodore Dreiser, Carl Van Vechten, George Jean Nathan, Konrad Bercovici, Ralph Barton..."

Her wit on her ninetieth birthday [August 20, 1985] is no less caustic. When I ask her for the secret of her longevity, her answer is direct: "If you think it's because I behaved myself when I was young, you're dead wrong!"

On the passing of one of her contemporaries, she remarks, "I avoided having lunch with her sixty years ago. I'm running out of people to hate."

I noted her one-sentence eulogy over the phone on the death of Mary

Pickford: "So she *was* human after all!"

On the occasion of her ninety-fourth birthday, Aileen Pringle is more serious: "At my age I have the choice of losing control of my mind or my body. Poor Charlie [Chaplin] never knew what was happening to him. But I do. I know I am falling apart. I have nurses here to bathe me, to dress me, to help me get from room to room. It isn't fun. I can barely see. I can't read the newspaper or watch television. I can't even answer my own telephone."

What becomes the final call, made ten days before her death, on December 16, 1989, is sadly prophetic.

"It isn't very good, Stuart. Sometimes I wake up and I don't know where I am. I don't know what day of the week it is. I am amazed I lasted this long. So many people have gone bye-bye. I'll probably be going bye-bye very soon…"

■

Aileen Pringle and Stuart Oderman.

Betty Bronson

1968: LOS ANGELES: THE HOLLYWOOD ROOSEVELT HOTEL

The banquet room is a sea of tablecloths, more difficult to navigate because the people are looking for their seat assignments, and trying to speak to the silent film celebrities who are present. Even the silent film celebrities are looking for the silent film celebrities, some of whom they haven't seen since the advent of sound. Luckily, it is an older crowd, many of whom are within the age bracket as the celebrities of their youth.

It is a little cool in the banquet room, and the soft, constant whirring of the air-conditioning sometimes makes some of the crowd go through a temporary visible adjustment. Betty Bronson doesn't have that problem. She has a lightweight, white cardigan which during the course of the dinner, she will gracefully drape over her shoulders.

"I'm not going to pretend I'm not a bit cold," she says to the six of us. "This room was always a problem. Luckily, they don't have me on the dais in front of everybody. You're always in full view, and somebody who wants to take your picture will dash over, snap you, and usually you are going to swallow a piece of meat, or wipe your lips with a napkin, and you'll look totally ridiculous when they show the picture to anyone. Sometimes people just like to watch you talking to somebody, or they try to read your lips, thinking they are going to hear something exciting, like a piece of gossip. I'm not really active in the film industry anymore, and the people who may remember me must have seen me when *Peter Pan* and *A Kiss For Cinderella* were made [1924, 1926].

"Those were children's movies which the family could see. When they show them today, the children who watch them are the *older* children

Betty Bronson.

from those days who watch with their own, young children. I don't have to worry about someone whispering *she was so glamorous when I first saw her.*

"Pat O'Brien, whenever he would show up at an occasional showing of his films, would tell the audience, 'I'm glad you came to watch, and notice how my hairline receded.' Then he would laugh. It was a wonderful ice-breaker.

"I don't know what audiences expect. It's rougher on the women, I think. We're always supposed to be perpetually glamorous." She points to one of the other actresses, and shrugs her shoulders before she turns to me, lowers her head, and covers her mouth.

"Stuart, I shouldn't say this, and I don't want my family to hear this, but I'm only here because of my grandchildren. I wanted them to see what I was doing when I was their age. Oh, they know I was *in old movies where actors didn't talk*, and they've only seen a few Charlie Chaplin things on television, and a few old stills of mine. But they've never seen any *films*. Luckily, they grew up like *real* children, and they're not teenagers yet, so seeing these films on a large screen might impress them.

"I always tell them I was working when I was their age, but it wasn't ever child's play. It was work *and* school. I had specific classes and tests, and there were tutors, and their job was to teach us math and history and give us homework. Sometimes we had little classes, sometimes we were being taught on our own. It was more supervised than in the early days, but there was always someone there to make sure we weren't being unsupervised and in potentially dangerous situations.

"*Peter Pan* was fun to make. There were a lot of children on the set, so we always had children to play with. Ernest Torrence, who played Captain Hook, was a big ham, acting in that melodramatic style, and Esther Ralston was a sweet lady. Because we had to be given some sort of education, there wasn't that much time to stay with the grown-ups, and possibly get in their hair. It was all very professional. It wasn't counselors with kids at summer camp.

"Because *Peter Pan* was produced at an American studio, they broke away from the British story line and inserted an American flag sequence, that may seem awkward and surprise those familiar with the play, but I think it was an attempt to make the story more universal, which it already was. It was never in the play.

"What always works with audiences all over the world is the sequence where Peter asks the audience to applaud. And they always do. Anyone who watches the film becomes so involved, they just see the title, and applaud.

"James M. Barrie, the author, liked the film. It was quite faithful to what he wrote. If there were any thoughts of using Maude Adams, the first actress to play Peter Pan, I never heard them. You also have to realize that when you are a child performer, you do what you were told to do. In the studio system, which I was a part of, you are told what to. Other people speak for you, and magazine writers, some of whom you've never met, will write what they think will make you more acceptable to an audience.

"James Barrie was so pleased with *Peter Pan* that he wanted only *me* to star in *A Kiss for Cinderella*, which was also a successful film. He also knew the importance of the dollar. Novels and stories, after their popularity, may be reprinted, but plays, if they are to enjoy any lasting popularity, *must* be seen on a stage. Motion pictures and theatrical plays are a collective experience for the audience. You read a novel or a story by yourself.

"I was a teenager when I was in *Peter Pan*, and I'm not going to say I never had a childhood, because I did. But what I wanted was the chance to be an adult. I was never sheltered, but after a while, it was almost a

Prince and the Pauper sort of life. Everyone wants to be everyone else. My grandchildren know I was in silent films, but they, like a lot of other people, don't know the day-to-day *business* of the *business*. I wouldn't want them to go into this kind of life. Popularity is a fleeting thing. Everyone does not spend their lives being chauffeured around, and being constantly stared at, and walking into flashing cameras. It's not real, and I always knew this. Don't misunderstand me. I don't regret anything I had, but I knew a time would come...

"I'll tell you what drove me out of the business: It wasn't fear of sound. It was two words: Al Jolson.

"The only reason he was in *The Jazz Singer* was due to Georgie Jessel, who played the Jolson role on stage. He thought that *talkies* had no future. What a wrong career move!

"*The Jazz Singer* brought Al Jolson back to the screen, his career was virtually over. Some people used to call him a *Mammy singer* who came out of a minstrel show tradition. He was an egomaniac, but, and I have to honestly say this: when he was singing in front of an audience he was truly electric.

"I was in *Sonny Boy* with him, and his ego was even bigger. I think he wanted everyone on the set to stand and applaud every time he entered a room. And thought he was the most desirable man on earth. If he could have pushed any supporting actor away from the eye of the camera, he would have gladly done so. He had all of the songs, and he would have said your lines, too. One of his films was called *The Singing Fool*. It was a wonderful title, but *The Total Fool* would have been more appropriate.

"*Are Parents People* was a nice little film. I played a young girl sent off to boarding school, because she doesn't want to live with either her mother or father, who are going through a divorce.

"Maybe I was a year or two older, but if I had filmed *Are Parents People* first, I don't think I would have been given the opportunity to be in *Peter Pan*.

"I'm rightfully partial to Peter Pan, because Peter is such a memorable character, and that is the one people remember. The other film is a nice programmer. A standard ingenue part.

"But I think the studio was trying to *age* me, if I can use that word.

"The Jolson experience soured me. He liked to humiliate the other players, and if I were a Joan Crawford or someone like that, I would have answered him in kind. But I'm not tough like that. I never was. And if I did, where would I go from there? Crawford was always a great pro, and she came on *tough*. But you had to respect her, because she was making it in a man's world, and that was the only way to last.

"I just wanted to get out. I wanted a regular *family* life. When the chance came to leave, I did. And I have no regrets.

"When I was offered *Blackbeard's Ghost* by the Disney organization, I took it. I was one of the old ladies, and it was fun to be back and working in a *family* film my *family* could see without being embarrassed.

"And today, we're going to see *Peter Pan*!

"It's a wonderful feeling to meet new generations, and for my grandchildren, it is a chance to see the *two* sides of Grandma…With their Grandma there to watch it with them!"

■

Betty Bronson and Stuart Oderman.

Patsy Ruth Miller

DECEMBER 1988: NEW YORK, THE MUSEUM OF MODERN ART

Twenty minutes before the six o'clock start of the evening's film, Lon Chaney in *The Hunchback of Notre Dame*, Patsy Ruth Miller, Lon Chaney's co-star who played Esmeralda, the gypsy girl, walks unaccompanied to her seat directly across the aisle from the piano.

It is as she wishes it: quiet, and without any fanfare.

Sixty-five years have passed since she had offered Quasimodo any water to quench his thirst after he has been brutally whipped.

Our eyes meet, she nods, and mouths a silent *good luck*, and my doubts have been confirmed. The passage of time has altered nothing: a *pro* is still a *pro*, even if she chooses to remain anonymous about it.

She, unlike the other film stars of that earlier era, is not gaudily dressed to call attention to herself. No Mae Murray requesting a window-table at high noon to be on exhibit to anyone passing by the Hollywood Roosevelt, hoping that she will be re-discovered.

Now that she returns my smile, and she knows what I do, what can I say? *In thirty years, I've only played one of your films? What else have you done that still exists, and hasn't been allowed to disintegrate with neglect?*

The silence between us is deafening. We are both waiting for the other to speak.

The ball is in my court, and it is my turn.

"What was Lon Chaney like?" I whisper. "I know you've..."

"...Been asked that same question," she says, "many, many times since I made that film [1923]."

133

Patsy Ruth Miller and Lon Chaney.

She takes a deep breath before she continues. What else can we talk about? The gathering December snow? Yesterday's rain?

As if the words are lines from a play she's been touring in for too long a period of time without any vacation, she continues, not bothering to see if I am listening. It is something that has to be told, and she is clearly tired of repeating herself. But she knows she must.

"I've made almost seventy-five films. I worked twice with Valentino

[*Camille* and *The Sheik*, both 1921] and very few people ask about him. I guess it's because Valentino's pictures were always about Valentino.

"Lon Chaney was the man of one-thousand faces. Each character wasn't the same character he played before. He packaged differently. Valentino was always the Lover. Women swooned over him, while men made fun of him and spread rumors. Maybe Valentino was too much of a threat. He was always synonymous with a good gallop over the hot burning sands, and into the tent until morning!

"Both men were gentlemen, and I can't tell who had the heavier burden: Valentino and torrid romance, or Lon Chaney and grotesque characterizations which took a toll of his health.

"On the set he was always *Mr.* Chaney. He never said anything to correct us, but his concentration and preparation were so intense, you naturally had to step aside for him.

"That harness he wore for *Hunchback* was quite heavy, and he *chose* to wear it from the moment he reported to the studio, until he left at the end of the day.

"He wrapped himself inside the character's head, as well as his physical body. He stayed by himself, because Quasimodo, being a hunchback was an outcast who was *forced* to stay by himself.

"He didn't ever give his *all* in rehearsals, but Lon Chaney's rehearsals had more intensity than most actors' finished products before the actual shooting began.

"When we blocked the scene when I'm supposed to give him the water he wanted, he played everything in silence, going through the motions, and then he suddenly yelled 'Water' with such pain, it scared us. We thought the harness had become too heavy, but we were afraid to approach him, because he shot a look at all of us that just said *Keep Away.*

"And that was what we did. We viewed him as Victor Hugo created him in the novel: an *outcast.*

"We wondered how he could even eat his lunch. He was always bent over, which must made it almost impossible to swallow very much. He had to have *cramps* when he removed his costume, and tried to take a few guarded steps.

"Paul Muni, in the thirties, was very similar: always staying in character, never socializing between takes, saving his *voice*, whereas Mr. Chaney worked in silents except for one sound film [*The Unholy Three*, 1930].

"I've always been a *working* actress, taking the parts in the pictures they gave me.

"It could have been worse, but whenever they show *The Hunchback of Notre Dame*, there I am: carrying the water!"

∎

Colleen Moore

LABOR DAY WEEKEND 1967: CHICAGO

This is not my first meeting with Colleen Moore. The first took place earlier that previous May at the Playboy Theatre in connection with a pre-television performance of a Chaplin documentary, *The Eternal Tramp*, written and produced by Harry Hurwitz, and narrated by Gloria Swanson. My score had been recorded. All I had to do was fly out there, and sit and watch, and hope the product was going to be televised on NET (National Educational Television), the precursor to PBS, and later ABC, in New York.

On that particular evening, June 5, 1967, my mind was concentrating on who would be in the audience, and was there a chance of my returning to Chicago?

In that audience were Woody Allen and June Havoc. Woody was appearing at Mister Kelly's, a Chicago nitery, and June was appearing at the Pheasant Run Playhouse in *George Washington Slept Here*, the Kaufman and Hart play.

In a crowded lobby Gloria Swanson introduced the two of us. "Stuart, this is Colleen Moore. He did the music, and he'll travel."

"You would come back here?" Colleen Moore asks.

There was a time when the very presence on the street of Colleen Moore would stop traffic. At premieres moviegoers would wait for hours just to get a fleeting glimpse of her as she was quickly ushered from her limousine and onto the red carpet and into the theatre. She was right next to Clara Bow as an *It* girl. Her leading men included Tom Mix, Antonio

Colleen Moore.

Moreno, John Barrymore, *and* Gary Cooper.

She would easily make the transition to sound, appearing opposite a young Spencer Tracy in *The Power and the Glory*.

And then, to everyone's surprise, she would willingly give up any opportunities for something as mundane and ordinary as marriage, a marriage to a widower with two young children.

"I was in my early thirties," Colleen said, "and I wasn't that big a success in the marriage department as I was on the screen. And I wanted something else besides a pile of scripts next to me on a chaise lounge by a swimming pool. I know every small town girl would have given everything to have what I had, but ultimately if you can't share it with someone, it's an empty, lonely life.

"You can't be glamorous all the time after a certain age. I had my dinners in all of the restaurants, and I danced in the best nightclubs.

"But now what? The guys who were getting older, were starting to look at girls who were younger. And the guys who were younger, well...

"I just felt it was time. Clara Bow, Betty Bronson, Connie Talmadge, Janet Gaynor, Greta Garbo: for whatever reasons they had, they left the business. Maybe it was marriage, a failure at sounding the way audiences thought you were going to sound, and Joan Crawford thought she sounded like a man in those early films, or just being tired of the constant isolation away from the cameras, and the way the studio would sort of *police* your off-hours away from the studio.

"Garbo, from the moment she same to California until she went back to New York in the early forties, was always a free spirit. She was very independent.

"Studios, especially MGM where Garbo worked, were first and foremost a *business*. How you behaved away from the camera was *your* business, but always within the boundaries of what wouldn't hurt *the* business.

"Garbo reporting at five in the morning?

"Garbo always leaving at five in the afternoon, whether or not her scenes were finished?

"Other players were a problem.

"Garbo? She had *mystique*!

"It was good for the *business*!

"When her last film, *Two-Faced Woman*, wasn't a success, and they realized Garbo's rhumba was no threat to Betty Grable's legs, she wisely left without any fanfare.

"Lillian's [Gish] last years at MGM, like Garbo's, were not her best. She didn't bring in the business, and she knew she couldn't be a flapper, even though her films had *prestige* and artistry all over them, while the body of my work was primarily standard flapper-fare.

"But my *Ella Cinders* and *Irene* were box-office successes.

"Her *Scarlet Letter* and *Romola* didn't set any cash registers ringing.

"I was always on-the-town somewhere. She wasn't.

"You didn't have to really create publicity for me at that point.

"When you signed a contract, the publicity department started to give you a biography. And the readers believed what they read in those days the way they do today. Usually it is supermarket tabloid publicity, and most of it isn't issued from the studio publicity department, because it isn't very flattering. If the tabloids were available in the supermarkets of the twenties, you'd never have a chance at a career. You'd be fired off the lot, the way they got rid of 'Fatty' Arbuckle!

"We'll create a biography right now.

"You're from Texas, or Montana, or Arizona? You're a farm girl.

"You're from New York? You were discovered working in a department store.

"If you were a Lillian Gish or a Mary Pickford, you had enough experience as a child touring in 10-20-30 melodramas.

"Theda Bara? She looked different. Her name spelled backwards was *Arab Death*. It made no difference that she was a nice Jewish girl from Ohio. She was a *mantrap*, and she had to be interviewed by *three* reporters at one time, because she cast such a bewitching spell, you couldn't help but succumb!"

She starts to laugh as the motel audience starts to enter the screening room. It is a small group of perhaps eighty people, many of whom carry flash-cameras and stills from *Lilac Time* with Gary Cooper.

A line, like an elementary school recess line, has formed itself near to the bridge table at which we sit. Someone brings over two glasses and a large pitcher of ice-water.

Colleen Moore graciously signs the photographs and answers a few questions about how she *discovered* Gary Cooper, and what a *real* man he was.

"For want of something to say about me, it was publicized that I was a dancer in Griffith's *Intolerance*. I knew how to dance, so why not place me in *Intolerance*, an epic Griffith film that had *hundreds* of dancers and extras?

"Of course, to anyone in the business, that was a signal or a code word that meant nobody knew what to say.

"The print we're showing of *Irene* is my own, and I travel with it. It was a popular long-running Broadway New York show, a musical, out of which came the standard 'Alice Blue Gown,' which was a favorite song played by hotel orchestras, and living room pianists all over the country.

"What is special about my print is the fashion show, which was an early experimentation in color. The color is somewhat faded, but it is still there, and you can get some idea of what it looked like when the film was originally released [1926].

"What I wish someone would find is the film of Edna Ferber's *So Big*. Edna Ferber was always writing about a specific section of the United States: *Show Boat* for the Mississippi, and *Giant*, which takes place in Texas.

"*So Big* was a wonderful dramatic role for me, as was *The Power and the Glory*, which I made with Spencer Tracy.

"The Tracy film was a sound film, and you can still find copies of it, and see what a powerhouse of an actor he was, even in those days.

"But *So Big* deserves to be seen, if it's available.

"I'm not just a flapper, and I never was a dancer in *Intolerance*!"

■

Colleen Moore and Stuart Oderman.

Jerry Devine

NEW YORK: THE BELASCO THEATRE, OCTOBER 24, 1973.
It is the opening night of *Children of the Wind*, an autobiographical play by Jerry Devine whose ca7reer began in silent films as a child actor in 1920 in *Over the Hill to the Poorhouse*, and until the advent of sound played juveniles, supporting the likes of Alice Brady (*Hush Money*), Elaine Hammerstein (*Remorseless Love*), Will Rogers (*The Headless Horseman*) and Thomas Meighan (*Tongues of Flame*), in addition to writing for radio (*The Shadow* and *Nick Carter, Master Detective*), before creating his original radio series, *The F.B.I. in Peace and War*, the only crime series given the approval of J. Edgar Hoover, Director of the Bureau.

I remind Jerry that I am familiar with his other plays: *Never Live Over a Pretzel Factory* and *The Amorous Flea*, and that, with the advent of technology, he is represented in two places at the same time: the Belasco Theatre opening, and uptown at a film society, a showing of his 1922 *The Headless Horseman*.

"Jerry, you can take a subway uptown to 1922, and come back to 1973," I tell him. "And you're still going!"

He laughs. "It means I'm not out on the balustrades yet!"

Diagonally across the street from Joe Allen's Restaurant on West Forty-sixth Street, and adjacent to a parking lot, is a brownstone that could have been the inspiration for O. Henry's *Furnished Room*. It exists in defiance of time.

"Let me look at this," Jerry says quietly to Janet, my wife, who has joined us for lunch when Jerry returns to New York the following spring.

143

"We used to have rooms here, on the top floor."

"Rooms?" I ask.

"Rooms," he says. "These were rooming houses that catered to what they used to call *transients*, traveling salesmen, who were called drummers and vaudevillians and musicians who were going to stay for only a short time until they went onto the next town.

"We stayed in a lot of these places, and we had to sneak in the food, and eat everything immediately and open the windows, because they didn't want any food smelling up the hallway. We'd open the window to keep the place aired. Landladies were always afraid of mice, and if anybody saw one, it would be hard to rent the rooms. Sometimes you had three or four in a room meant for two, which meant one or two had to sleep on the floor, and we'd have to sneak them in and out.

"Sometimes, if you returned to the rooming house a few months later, you had to hope the landlady or the manager liked you, and you weren't any problem. No noise, no fights.

"You hung your wash on the roof, and if you had any vacant space you played ball there. No street traffic to worry about.

"I remember running into the Mershon Brothers here. The Mershon Brothers, I think, were French acrobats, or whatever it was that they did. I think their names were Louis or Pierre. Something like that. French names, you know. And they did tumbling.

"Louis, I think it was, used to cook in their room. I don't know what it was. It was meat, and potatoes, and vegetables all at once. And they used this pot that they carried with them.

"I don't know who did the shopping, or where they found time to get the food, but one day, when the window was open, I smelled whatever it was, and they gave me some in a bowl. I honestly couldn't identify what it was and they said it was something like *glop*.

"That's what it sounded like: glop.

"Seeing that house brought everything back, and I haven't seen that house in over fifty years. Or maybe more.

"You can't run away from your past, or maybe it can't run away from you."

In the summer, we are invited for dinner at Jerry and his wife Marylin's home in Beverly Hills. It has a backyard, but there is no tennis court or obligatory swimming pool, which he dismisses as *Hollywood crap*. It is a house that is meant to be lived in, not a showpiece for an *Architectural Digest* or a television interview. Any performance memorabilia from the days of silent films, radio, or theatre can be found in the den, competing for space with books and scripts that crowd the floor-to-ceiling bookcases in every possible available space.

There is a theatrical Playbill with a play title and *James* Devine that calls for attention.

"My father," Jerry says quietly, "the inspiration for *Children of the Wind*. A competent alcoholic-Irish-self-destructive man, if I can say that phrase in one breath: alcoholic-Irish-self-destructive man, who, after he got the job, proceeded to drink himself out of it.

"It was a pattern, and you have to come from that kind of background to understand it. He never spoke about any formal schooling. I don't think too many people had any formal schooling after the eighth grade. You had to go to work and help your family.

"*I never had a childhood.* Never could do what the other kids did. Never could have any kind of kid's life.

"I had to be the wage-earner, because he clearly wasn't. And the ironic thing about him is that he still could get some kind of work in the theatre, doing his eight shows a week. And then when it seemed to look as if the play was going to have a sustained run, my father then proceeded to do whatever he could do to destroy himself.

"The theater was always an insecure profession. In those days, you never knew how long you were going to last; I heard the backstage stories about Jeanne Eagles, but she somehow managed to get on, and do her shows. And I think that was a lot of hype. I saw her in *Rain*, and she was brilliant. She may have chewed the scenery on some days, but that often happens when you get trapped in a long run, which is a blessing and a curse.

"I never had a childhood, because I was looking after my father.

"When we had hard times, *I* was the breadwinner. I was supporting my family in those rooms on what *I* made. I was *pushed* into this business!"

"But you were able to get work," I said.

"That was the *blessing*! I went to a professional children's school. In my class were Milton Berle and Monica Lewis' brother.

"I happened to have talent, and was good at what I had to do!

"I got a copy of *The Headless Horseman*, and I ran it for my wife

Marylin and our daughter, Brigitte. They were watching it, because they may have heard me talk about it. I have a very critical eye, and I can honestly say that I thought that kid was pretty good. He didn't over-gesture the way a lot of young kids did in those days. He was quite modern."

"Can you see yourself with two different points of view?" I ask.

He nods. "Always," he answers. "How else can I be so objective…Did you ever come across *Remorseless Love*? Elaine Hammerstein is in it."

"I've never seen it. I think it's gone."

"A talented, very sad girl, whose family forced her into films when she was twelve years old. The ironic thing is that she had *talent*. And she had the Hammerstein name. Her father was Arthur. You couldn't get better credentials than that. She did stage and films, and she wanted no part of it. Elaine Hammerstein didn't like the business.

"Her cousin, Oscar who wrote with Richard Rodgers, told her to stand up for herself, but she couldn't do it. When we did *Remorseless Love*, she must have been in her early twenties, and I was still a kid, but I had a crush on her, and when she told me she hated the business, and it was all she ever did, and *she never had a childhood, well…*

"Did you ever come across John Barrymore's *Sherlock Holmes*?"

I told him there was a print at the Eastman House in Rochester.

"That was some set," he laughed. "I had a small part, I think the juvenile's name was Billy. [Charles] Chaplin played the role on stage.

"After I was finished with my scenes, they would send *the kid* [he points to himself] to the drugstore to get a 'bottle of gin for Mr. Barrymore,' and to hurry back quickly.

"I was filming and running!

"I'll tell you what it was like being a child actor: your life wasn't your own. You probably had some relative who was in the business, and there may have been hard times. If you had a theatre background, you knew what it was all about, and many times you were the breadwinner. Whatever you made supported the family. There were no labor laws, and you often worked long hours that sometimes went into the night…and then you had to be back the next day. You never had a childhood. I know I never had a childhood.

"I remember being in one film where they needed a shot of me swimming in the water. It was late in the day, the water was freezing-cold, and they weren't satisfied with how the scene was going. The director wanted the scene to go a certain way, and I was constantly being shoved into the water. Over and over. Into the water, swim a few feet, then come back, get out, get toweled, and stand shivering and waiting until they could shoot the scene again.

"I don't think it even was used in the final cut. So many films had scenes that were taken out.

"I remember I hated it, and I had no choice but to do it. That was the way it was. And I wished I could be anyplace else but near that water. Other kids must have better lives, but I had to be the breadwinner.

"I'll tell you: I *never* had a childhood!"

Constance Talmadge

MAY 1968: NEW YORK: THE BOOTH THEATRE

Some times you know or think you know a lot about people, because other people talk about them: where they go and who is seen with them.

It sells newspapers.

Like the Gabors (Zsa Zsa, Eva, Magda) of the fifties, the Talmadges (Constance, Norma, Natalie) of the twenties were also pursued by the news media. They had minimal acting talent, but they were *loved* by the camera, and their films had the sisters in escapist locales in the latest fashions.

Both the Gabors and the Talmadges had domineering mothers who instructed their beautiful daughters to be ambitious in their pursuit of the Three M's: money, men, and marriage.

"If my sisters and I had any success in the movies," elegantly dressed Constance Talmadge tells me, "it was because of my mother. *Mother Talmadge*, as she liked to be called, made all of our decisions for us: what to wear, where we should be seen, and with *whom* we should be seen. College men were all very nice to have as good friends, but we had to ask ourselves the obvious questions: where were these boys going, and what kind of future would we have? After all, our mother had taken us *this* far, and it was time for us to see how we could provide for her, now that she was getting older, *as we all were*.

"Dorothy Gish said we were our mothers' meal tickets, but Lillian always defended her mother, not that we ever attacked them, by saying we had arrived where we had arrived, because of our mothers. Our mothers paved the way for us to earn a living, and were wise enough to be

Norma and Constance Talmadge.

always on hand to protect us from unscrupulous men.

"Our mothers were opposites. I worked with Lillian in *Intolerance* [1916] for a few days, and at the end of the day's shooting, Lillian and her mother went home. Dorothy was probably off somewhere with one of the guys.

"My sisters and I didn't always stay together, but we knew we had to keep out of trouble, as they used to say. But *trouble* was never explained. Trouble in those days, and trouble *these* days have two different meanings…

"Both Mother Gish and Mother Talmadge were simple homemakers who saw us as the key to their futures. There weren't many avenues of opportunity open to women, single women, those days. And even less opportunities were available to single women with three daughters. Daughters our age were very vulnerable.

"What could simple, uneducated women do? Work in a factory, or go out West and look for a husband you hoped would stay with you, or become a prostitute. You know the saying, 'Heaven will protect the working girl?' That's okay, if she's *working*.

"I know the words women's lib and feminist are tossed casually around, and some people, men and women, laugh and think it's a joke, but they weren't around when we were trying to eke out a living and wonder where our next meal was coming from.

"You go to your library and find [Theodore] Dreiser's *Sister Carrie* and *Jennie Gerhardt* were not that far removed from the truth. A girl had to keep her wits about her if she wanted to survive. Going on the stage or into the movies were as lowly a way of earning a living as standing under a street-lamp. Actors and *especially* actresses were not acceptable ways for people to earn a living. For ladies, young ladies, it was little better than being a tart or a streetwalker, no matter how much you were chaperoned by your mothers. The idea of a young girl putting herself *on display*…

"A young girl's life, no matter what economic strata she came from, was pretty much pre-determined at birth. America, in those days, was a very class conscious society. First generation wealth was always seen as vulgar.

"But not the second or third generation, if you held onto it, and were able to make the proper personality adjustments! If you acquire money, and the situation and circumstances may be a little underhanded, you can practically rewrite your life if: do not call negative attention to yourself, read books and be able to discuss them intelligently on a conversational level, frequently go to the opera, and *not* get a box seat, and dress well, but not in an ostentatious way.

"We were the products of what the fan magazines wrote about us. Some of us actually became what they said.

"Archie Leach was a stage actor, a trained tailor, and he could also walk on those stilts in circus troupes when the work came up. When he left New York for California, he could go into a tailor's shop, and buy bolts of cloth which he would cut and sew to his own measurements.

"The next day he would walk down Hollywood Boulevard at high noon, the best time for anyone to see you, and go into an expensive hotel, find a seat in the lobby, unfold the newspaper he was carrying under his arm, and proceed to read, completely oblivious to whoever might be watching. You couldn't help but stare at him, and none of the desk clerks would ask him to leave. He was attracting too much attention.

"When Archie became Cary, he would tell that story, and then laugh, 'I'd like to *be* Cary Grant!'

"From the beginning, he was always a gentleman, and he *looked* like what you thought a movie star should look like!

"Anytime I meet people, they always mention the Babylonian sequence from Griffith's *Intolerance* [1916], Lillian [Gish] is only in the mother-rocking—the-baby-interludes. And she would always say that.

"*Intolerance* was the spectacle that set the standard for future spectacle. But it didn't make the money Mr. Griffith thought it would. He was only able to make *Intolerance* because *The Birth of a Nation* was such a huge success.

"Mr. Griffith was a wonderful artist, but he had absolutely no business sense when it came to money. Had he made *Intolerance* first, which would have been an impossibility because *The Birth of a Nation* was quite long, and quite a financial risk, the studio would have gone bankrupt, and would have been considered unemployable.

"On the set of *Intolerance* Lillian's mother was always present to watch over her, as my mother was present to watch over me!

"Mother Gish had two daughters, but they were quite different. Lillian was the serious one. In every film she did, she was always the 'damsel-in-distress,' and Dorothy had the bigger stretch: comedy and drama with equal ease. Dorothy was a much better actress than Lillian, but she never wanted a career the way Lillian did.

"Dorothy was a great party-girl. She was always going to parties, while Lillian stayed with her mother. When Dorothy and I went out on the town, or to parties with men, we never had a chaperone; Lillian, even when she would spend an evening with Mr. Griffith, always made sure Mother Gish saw them. For *part* of the evening…

"I don't know anything about any *romance* between the two of them. I read about this, but I was there, and I never saw anything. But I had my own beaus, and so did Dorothy! And Mr. Griffith was *married!*

"Dorothy and I, on one of the times we were with our beaus, thought of something quite *daring*.

"We both wanted to elope, but we were afraid to do it on our own. We were both making money, we were both supporting our mothers. So why not do something for ourselves?

"We double-dared each other: I will if you will...

"This was in the twenties, and eloping was the most daring thing you could do. And we could rid ourselves out of being constantly 'advised' by our mothers.

"So John (my first husband: I had four), and I eloped! And Dorothy and Jim [actor James Rennie] eloped...

"Of course, it was a mistake, and it proved our mothers were right. Dorothy's marriage lasted longer, I think. I'm not much on dates like that.

"But I say this in hindsight: it was probably the first time either of us ever took the initiative to do something on our own. To make our own decisions! Maybe if we were brought up like other children, instead of reporting to a studio instead of a school, things would have turned out differently.

"In no way am I bitter. I've had a very nice, nice life. I never went into the sound era. I never went into radio or summer stock. I saved my money, and my sisters saved their money, and our mother showed us how to invest it for our benefit.

"I'm out of the picture business...a long time. And I don't regret it. It was fun, but I never had a *regular* life. I was always on-the-go, and while it's nice to meet people so many, many years afterwards, it was a very demanding lifestyle. It looks glamorous, but it was never anything but work. You were a moneymaker or not a moneymaker.

"When sound came in, those who were lucky, were often in supporting roles, and as the years went by, and you got older, you sometimes had to be working for studios who were fly-by-night, and you hoped your check would clear the bank.

"Or sometimes someone remembered you and you were called back to do crowd scenes.

"I didn't want that. I didn't want to go back to the bottom of the ladder, and try to smile my way through, and hope someone would remember me. I made my money, I held onto my money, and I knew when to leave.

"Nobody was ever going to say, 'Constance Talmadge? I remember her. What's she doing now?'

"I'm a hospital *volunteer* worker, and I *don't* get paid. I like what I do, and I like my hours, and I like the people I work with, and nobody young knows or understands what I used to do, and I'm not ever going to be an object of sympathy in some tabloid, and be discussed in beauty parlors by people who never heard of me.

"That's not for me. I have wonderful stepchildren, and nephews."

■

Constance Talmadge.

Lois Wilson

1970: NEW YORK: THE METROPOLITAN MUSEUM OF ART

Lois Wilson is sitting in an aisle seat directly across from the piano. Like the hundreds of others who attended the showing of Cecil B. DeMille's *Manslaughter* (1922), in which she appeared with Leatrice Joy, she is applauding.

When Leatrice Joy, seated next to her, motions for the two of them to stand, the audience roars, to their surprise.

In true Hollywood fashion, they exchange hugs, and then wave at the audience.

"I'm happy that I'm here," Lois Wilson says to me. "And I'm happy that Leatrice is here, and the *two* of us are here almost fifty years later! Who would have thought we'd be living so long? And still be in touch? And still be friends!

"We knew each other *slightly*, but Mr. DeMille called us separately, and said the same words: 'Will you do this film if I can get...,' and we both jumped at the chance. Both good parts, and we knew it would be a lot of fun, which it was!

"I was never a child actress forced to tour all over the country like Lillian [Gish] or Mary [Pickford], sometimes with adults I never knew, to support my family. I was never very good copy for the movie magazines or the newspapers.

"Whenever I was asked to talk about myself, I would tell them the truth: that I came from Pennsylvania, and I was an elementary schoolteacher for a short time, and then I went to Chicago and then Los Angeles as part of Lois Weber's Company. Lois was a very religious person, a Christian Scientist, and one of the first woman directors in the film business. Women directors were nothing new, but Lois Weber took screen credit for it.

"It's unfortunate that a lot of her work wasn't preserved properly. You didn't have what we call *revivals* in those days. You had first-run features in the

Lois Wilson.

metropolitan areas, and second-run features in the more rural areas. They weren't what became 'B' features, because the first-run films did eventually go to the small towns. The 'B' features couldn't compete with the big studio products, but it was possible to have a sort of career in the 'B' features, but you always went back to the theatre and the tours.

"I wish *The Great Gatsby* were available. I played Daisy in the original release [1926], and I haven't seen it since then. I don't even know if it exists. The film was an adaptation of the F. Scott Fitzgerald novel, and the play by Owen Davis.

"I don't think Fitzgerald translates well to the screen. So much of his writing is interior, with wonderfully descriptive phrases that are difficult for a camera to pick up. And we were working without sound.

"Even in sound Fitzgerald is rough to take from page to screen, which has the advantage of the spoken word. You don't *speak* thoughts.

"Does anyone remember or read Zane Grey? He wrote westerns, and they were always a staple, like mysteries. There was always an audience for them, primarily armchair travelers who responded to his authentic descriptions, and the great ability to keep the story moving.

"I know that Zane Grey will never be in the class of a Tolstoy, but none of his books that were filmed, and there were many, ever lost money at the box office. *The Vanishing American*, in which I co-starred with Richard Dix, was the sort of *Guess Who's Coming to Dinner* with a Navajo Indian, who falls in love with a white schoolteacher.

"I'm very proud of *Miss Lulu Bett*, which was a Pulitzer Prize play on Broadway. Luckily, I played the lead. Even in those days very few of the New York players were fortunate to play their creations on the screen. I don't think it was a rivalry. It was a case of dollars and sense business. Who will bring in the paying customers? It's a different attitude. When Lillian and I played on Broadway in *I Never Sang for My Father* [1968], neither of us was chosen to play our parts when the play was filmed.

"*Work* is *work*. You hope you've done something people will remember.

"That's what this profession is about: being remembered, and being remembered well.

■

Claire Windsor

JULY 1969: LOS ANGELES, A PRIVATE HOME

If you travel enough between San Francisco and Los Angeles, and are socially and culturally observant, you cannot help but notice two essentially disparate cultures, each with its own set of mores.

In San Francisco you have the theatre, and the symphony, and very fine restaurants. The entertaining is done *outside* the home.

Los Angeles has all of the same amenities, *but* the entertaining, if it is not connected with television or motion pictures, is done *inside* the home.

Since the time silent films began to be a vital part of the economy and were called *the industry,* a term that exists even now, *where* you lived added to the sell-ability of the house, in addition to its historic significance. Hence, there is the Clara Bow house on Roxbury; the William Desmond Taylor bungalow on North Alvarado; and, of course, Pickfair and Falcon's Lair, the dwellings of Douglas Fairbanks and Mary Pickford, and Rudolph Valentino and Natacha Rambova. You dined out only if you wanted to be seen. You entertained at home to celebrate the conclusion of a film assignment, or if you wanted to be indiscreet and not be the subject of any gossip columnist.

At the Queens Road residence of press agent and sometimes producer Ed Finney ("I discovered 'Tex' Ritter, when he was singing on a small local radio station"), you are likely to also receive a mini-history of his home, which he will tell you "was the home of William Powell when he was married to Carole Lombard. Did you ever see a sunken living room? That was the sign of class in those days, a sunken living room. Real class."

What is the evening's entertainment after the dinner and drinks for a crowd who is connected directly in all kinds of capacities with the *industry*?

Movies!

You sit and watch movies! New movies, old movies, and sometimes *silent movies*.

And when there's a silent film pianist there from New York...

Amongst the guests is silent film star Claire Windsor, who starred for Goldwyn and Metro Pictures when they were separate studios, before they merged and became MGM: Metro-Goldwyn-Mayer!

Discovered in 1920 by Lois Weber, one of the first female directors and producers able to sustain a career, even for a respectable time in what was a man's *industry*, Claire became a Wampas Baby Star two years later.

"I can honestly assure you, Stuart," the still dazzlingly beautiful Claire quietly says in perfectly resonating tones, "we were *never* babies!"

"The feature of the evening is *The Kid*, starring Charlie Chaplin," Ed Finney announces.

"I used to go around with him," Claire tells the living room audience. "We spent a few evenings together. No more than five or six, I think. I forgot about them, and when I heard I was mentioned in Lita's book (Lita Grey, Chaplin's second wife), I was *un*pleasantly surprised. Some people will do anything to sell a book. I heard she mentioned a lot of girls. And not very kindly. I thought Charlie was very charming...What's the short?" she asks Ed.

"Film clips," Ed answers. "A compilation of silent film clips from the old days. *The Stars at Work and Play*."

"An original title," Claire says. "Please don't show me *at play*."

The lights are dimmed, the projector is turned on, and we see candid shots of Claire Windsor arriving at some premiere in a limousine outside Grauman's Chinese Theatre. The audience applauds, and the scene dims. Moments later, we see Claire Windsor arriving at another premiere, dressed quite differently. Again, the audience applauds. And then, there is *color* footage of an older Claire in a limousine. This time she is arriving at an unidentified park.

This time, instead of waving to the large sidewalk, she merely gets out of the car, and turns and gestures to the grass.

"Do you know where you are?" Ed asks.

"No, but it looks like a lovely park. I guess this is an example of being *at play*. Look how the camera just takes in everything: the face, my dress,

Claire Windsor.

my shoes. I don't think this cameraman ever shot any features. He may have been a newsreel photographer covering fashion shows. Lord knows, there were enough of them."

Claire Windsor, born Olga Kronk ("not a very glamorous name, is it?") in Kansas, the winner of a local beauty contest. The prize was a Hollywood contract.

"You really couldn't take those Hollywood contracts too seriously. Girls were flocking to Hollywood by bus and train every single day. Every girl was going to be a star.

"It was sad, because most of those girls had no talent. You can see prettier girls on the beaches at Malibu and Santa Monica. After a few months of really not getting anywhere, these girls realize the only pictures they are going to be in are the ones by their friends with their cameras!

"Winning a beauty contest was like the old story about Lana Turner being discovered at the drugstore soda fountain. She may have been only seventeen, but she had her portfolio of glossies!

"In the silent days I was a working actress, and I paid my union dues, and I stayed in pictures until the very early fifties.

"Luckily for me, I was able to do stage work when the opportunity came up, though not very often because I was in pictures, and that took up a lot of my time.

"My worst experience was going on tour with Al Jolson in *Wonder Bar* in the early thirties. It had been a success on Broadway, because Al Jolson was such a wonderful performer. Very friendly, very personable -until you had to be onstage with him. If you got more laughs or were able to take the attention away from him, even for a minute, he was a horror!

"He had made his theatrical comeback in *Wonder Bar*, and a road tour was certainly in order.

"If Georgie Jessel, who originated the role on Broadway in *The Jazz Singer*, hadn't turned *down* the chance to do the film, I don't know if we would have the same film industry. Jessel didn't know the camera the way Al Jolson instinctively did. There wasn't supposed to be any dialogue of any extent, but Jolson just 'ad-libbed' something, and everything took off!

"Working with Jolson for eight shows a week was another matter. We used to say the show shouldn't be called *Wonder Bar*, but *Wonder Why*.

"There was a backstage story about Jolson that Georgie Jessel loved to tell. Al Jolson, in the midst of all of his success with his comeback in *The Jazz Singer*, suddenly realized he wasn't well received by a lot of the Hollywood crowd. He received offers to perform, but nobody was asking him to very many dinners. He asked Georgie why, and Georgie answered, 'Because you're a rotten son of a bitch!'

"When I was on stage with Jolson, night after night, eight shows a week, I had no choice but to *listen* to his lines. He would roll his eyes at the audience, as if to tell them a joke was coming. I thought when he sang he brayed like a jackass, but the audience loved him, and it was because of him, like him or not, *we were working*!

"I'll tell you who was a lovely person, but quite tragic. I never worked with her, but when you saw her, your heart just went out to her: Helen Morgan.

"Rouben Mamoulian told me she was quite generous to everyone. She had a bedside scene with a little girl, and she *gave* the scene to her, just gave it. And it was a better scene, too! Helen Morgan was a good singer, and an actress. The film was *Applause*. There are prints of it still around.

"I'd give anything if somebody could locate a print of *Rupert of Hentzau* [1923]. Bert [husband Bert Lytell] and I were co-starring, and I'd like my grandchildren to see it.

■

Jackie Coogan

1980: LOS ANGELES: THE BAR OF THE LOS ANGELES HILTON HOTEL

At one on the morning, somebody is still chortling through a few movie tunes from the forties, oblivious to the dim lights, and the lack of patronage. An overused bar rag, darkened in a few places from being swiped across the counter whenever someone enters, is probably the only way the barman has of calling to a few customers that drinks are still available. There are no ladies at the bar, and the few senior hopefuls are getting ready to leave, reaching into the potato chip bowl or the pretzel bowls in an effort to cover any liquor smells, and to settle their stomachs before the dark ride home.

Jackie Coogan, whose long career goes back to *The Kid*, playing opposite Charlie Chaplin in 1920, through the sound era, and into the television era.

"A good, and not always so good a life, but I've come out on top," he likes to say, given the attention and new generations of fans *The Addams Family* has brought him.

He is seated at one of the empty tables, and he gestures for me to join him. It is a sometimes successful ploy. Nobody will come over, or stay very long, if they see he is holding a conversation.

Occasionally he rises to acknowledge a compliment, shake hands with the well-wisher, and then return to the topic of conversation. In this case, the number of miles on his speedometer had caught his attention. Foolishly, when he parked his car, he gave the keys to the attendant. The car is still in the same space, he tells me, but there is a small, noticeable scratch

165

over the right rear wheel. And the mileage had increased a little too much for just being 'moved a little.'

"The insurance will take care of it," Jackie Coogan says. "I check on everything, especially when I have to use a public parking lot. It comes with the territory. You want to drive Jackie Coogan's car without Jackie Coogan's permission? Okay. Then you'll pay for Jackie Coogan's insurance!"

"Would you have let him?" I ask.

"Let him *what*? Drive my car? No way, Jose!"

"It's *The Addams Family*'s fault! I'm in living rooms, and barrooms, and bedrooms, and gas stations, and motel rooms. I'm like part of the public conscience. The public thinks they *own* you…And in a way, they do.

"But this is a different generation. In the old days, they wanted you to sign a photograph or pose with you. Now you get asked opinions on everything. I'm an actor, not a politician, or investments counselor, or marriage counselor.

"I'm used to meeting people who stare at me before they speak. And I know what they're thinking. *What happened to the little boy with the Buster Brown haircut who was taken care of by Charlie Chaplin in* The Kid?

"And my answer is very simple: *The Kid* grew up!

"I can classify the two types of mail I get. And I answer all of my mail.

"I get Chaplin questions from the film students and *Addams Family* mail.

"The Chaplin mail is always going back to the making of *The Kid*. I wish I knew all of the answers. I was a *Kid* myself when I made that film [1920]. Who knew back then, especially a six-year-old, that he'd talking to film *majors* who *study* film?

"I'm from a generation when movies were new. Movies were young. I was totally unaware of went on outside in the real world. I just had to be ready for the studio car when it came to pick me up early in the morning when it was still dark outside

"I was sheltered and protected, and *watched*. Always *watched*. My salary supported my family, and I won't say anymore about that. I've been through it too many times, and I can't get excited about what was done.

"What was done, was done. And I can't re-live it. It has taken me my whole life to try to forget it, but sometimes people ask *financial* questions and I can read their *eyes*.

Charlie Chaplin and Jackie Coogan.

"When I tell them I was *working* when most kids were playing and going to school, the questioners back away.

"I like when they call this business an *industry*. That's what it always was: an industry. Studios were factories. They manufactured a product: fantasy on a daily, weekly, or monthly basis. It depended on how often you went to the movies.

"But we were always working. The public's fantasy was our reality.

"Motion pictures were the public's fantasy, and our lives were the studio's fantasy. They created an off-screen persona for us. They created a *biography* for us; where we were born, who our parents were, our childhood, how we were discovered.

"Some of that stuff was true, but they would embellish it a little. "[D.W.] Griffith didn't even want his actors to have names or billing. When wonderful Mabel Normand's early work was shown in England, her name was *Muriel Fortesque*!

"The studio ran your life. When you were under contract, it was a *contract*! You were told where to go, where to be seen, what to wear, and what people you should date, and it even went into marriages.

"In the silent days, it was quite a while before the public was told Francis X. Bushman and Beverly Bayne were *married*! They were 'the screen lovers!' And young girls, they were the film magazine readers, would have been shattered. They thought motion picture actors were Gods from Mount Olympus!

"And in a way, they were! For some like Charlie [Chaplin], a publicity machine was a good thing. But even he made the newspapers, and the publicity machines weren't always able to protect him.

"Charlie always liked young girls. He met Lita Grey when she was twelve, but, being a gentleman, he waited two years, until she was fourteen...

"And then he married her...

"For the sake of the baby.

"His autobiography is honest and frank, and I thought he was very kind to his wives.

"Lita Grey's book [*My Life With Chaplin*] is the *more* truthful side of the story. *She* gets into the sexual details, where Charlie simply said that he had some from the marriage.

"He was being a gentleman, while she was being vengeful *again*.

"After all those years! To still drag it up!

"What was it that Shakespeare said about *a woman scorned*?

"Why did those old stars last so long?" I ask.

Jackie Coogan rubs his hand across his forehead, and looks in the direction of the pianist. His tip glass still holds the same five-dollar bill since we came. Clearly it is not a good night.

"Quantity," he answers. "You were under contract, and they worked you around the clock. You were a marketable product. Cagney, Joan Blondell, William Powell, Humphrey Bogart: they made a lot of those films sometimes in less than two weeks.

"The same way in the silent days: features and two-reelers to round out the program. You just went from one to the other. No television competition to worry about. You had to turn out a product which would be shipped.

"In those days you paid for a performance, and going to the movies once or twice a week for a guy and his girl was a special occasion. The films opened in the major cities first at the first-run houses. Then they were sent to the neighborhood theatres. You *paid* for a performance. You didn't sit home in your underwear, drinking a beer by yourself.

"You paid for a performance, and you got one, if the actor had any ability. For a girl, in the film industry, it was always different, but don't read me wrong. The big audience was women, but guys would go in if the lady looked good: Ava Gardner, my ex-wife Betty Grable, Rita Hayworth. All gorgeous ladies - and don't forget Lana Turner.

"World War II was in the forties, and the publicity photos that went out to GI's was a tremendous morale booster.

"She's not in that gorgeous class, but I'll include Joan Crawford. She was a tiger from the minute she got off the train Harry Rapf brought her on. She was a Black Bottom dancer. My father was directing a picture she was in, and she couldn't *cry*.

"Take after take, walking down those stairs, she wouldn't cry. Finally, my father ordered everybody to clear the set.

"Everyone left, but I was able to hide in one of the corners.

"My father told Joan to walk up to the last step, turn slowly around, and look directly at him at the bottom of the steps.

"'Okay, Joan, just listen to what I say. When I call for *action*, I want you to walk slowly down the stairs, just looking at *me*. At nobody else! Only me. Are you ready? Only me! *Action!*'

"As Joan started to walk slowly down those steps, my father took out a clipboard, and began to read the name of every man she had been involved with, even if only for one night. You could see the surprise on her face, but he told her to *keep walking*, not to lose her concentration.

"And he continued read: name after name, place after place.

"She started to cry, but she kept going down those steps.

"By the time she arrived at the bottom step, Joan Crawford had cried a good five-hundred feet.

"She looked up at my father, and gave him one of those Joan Crawford I-hate-you-looks. She despised what he had done. To mention just about every single involvement. And there were many.

"The film kept rolling, and then my father yelled, and this was without sound for the entire sequence, 'Cut!'

"And that's why Joan Crawford is a real pro! And that's why she lasted!"

■

Madge Bellamy

1980: LOS ANGELES: THE LOS ANGELES HILTON HOTEL

Unless you were told in advance who she was, you wouldn't probably recognize Madge Bellamy. Like Patsy Ruth Miller in New York, Madge arrived without any fanfare, and quietly walked to the vacant seat near the piano.

With her is a lady companion, a next door neighbor, who introduced the two of us, and whispered, "I want Madge to be with people who remember her. She thinks she's forgotten, because not too many of her films are still in existence. She also doesn't understand why people would fly to Los Angeles to spend a weekend watching old movies around the clock."

What Madge's friend said was partially true. Film buffs are like art collectors, and first-edition collectors, and any special group that meets at a specific time in a specific place to discuss the people for whom they have a great respect: The Anthony Trollope Society, The Wizard of Oz Society, The Sons of the Desert (Laurel and Hardy), ad infinitum.

Madge Bellamy has never been collected to the degree of a Lillian Gish or a Greta Garbo or a Judy Garland. She was never the symbol of an era like Clara Bow. Nor was she exotic like Louise Brooks.

Madge Bellamy was simply *there*, even though her name or few available films rarely will be included in a semester's film study course.

Her *Lorna Doone*, perhaps the film for which she is most remembered, is not *her* favorite. "A costumer," she will tell you. "Read the book, if you must. Why do people always mention *Lorna Doone?*"

Because it is probably the only thing you ever did that is still around, I want to tell her.

Suddenly she smiles, "You know I was in the first national touring company of James M. Barrie's *Dear Brutus*? I'm essentially a theatre person. Most of us were. We came from stock companies or touring companies who wound up in California. So they stayed, because studios were cropping up all over the place, and the pace was easier. You had twenty-four hours of beaches, sand, and sun. And houses were cheap, if you were willing to live out of the movie area."

A fan walks up to her and asks, "Do you think they'll run *White Zombie* tonight?

"*I'll* run first," she answers.

Her friend explains, "That's another one she dislikes. That old horror film from the thirties. Poor sound, and Bela Lugosi doing a pathetic parody of himself."

"*Everything* Lugosi did after *Dracula* was a parody," Madge chimes in. He thought he was charming, and when you see his earlier films, he actually *was*.

"But *Dracula*," she shakes her head. "What a pity. Monster movies…Good moneymakers, but a trap for actors if they think that is all you can do.

"Boris Karloff fared a little better, even though he was still Frankenstein to a lot of people, like Lon Chaney was the Wolf Man.

"Those films made money, but nobody ever really took those later ones very seriously as an art form.

"John Carradine? A wonderful actor. But he did his share of horror films.

"You made a good living, and you could certainly pay the rent. They've become classics, I suppose, and I could have made a few more, but what would I be doing? Scream?"

The lights dim, and the screen lights up: MADGE BELLAMY! The audience applauds, and Madge removes a handkerchief from her purse.

The title flashes: *Love Never Dies*. Madge, no longer sitting ramrod straight, shifts in her seat, finds a comfortable position, and settles back.

After the credits, she leans forward and whispers. "I haven't seen this in years."

Throughout the showing, she will comment: "A lot of takes on that scene…I was out the night before. You know: *OUT!*"

I continue to play, hoping I can concentrate on the film, which I am playing for the first time. No chance to preview, not even a one- or two-line summary.

The commentary on Bellamy's past starts again. She is talking to the piano player, but we're not in a bar. "Drinking…God knows what, as long as it went down easy.

"Sometimes I got to the studio on time, and that was because I had a chauffeur. Some of us had that privilege, a chauffeur. It didn't last forever."

She looks at the screen. An older character actor playing a mailman is standing outside her picket fence. He hands her a letter, and then tips his hat before he leaves to deliver more mail further down the country. It is a sweet country scene, the type that was probably duplicated in hundreds of films of this type.

Against the flickering light from the screen, Madge starts to weep. "That nice old man. The mailman. I never learned his name. Do you know who he is? He must be dead by now. I think the others are gone, too.

"And I'm *older* now than that actor who played the mailman!"

Her companion squeezes her arm, hoping Madge will stop whispering.

Madge wipes another tear away. "I guess this is the reward for outliving your contemporaries. She can see them, but you can't hear them, or talk to them!

"That song you're playing: 'Just a Song at Twilight.' It makes me cry. So many of those old songs do: 'If You Were the Only Girl in the World,' 'That Old Gang of Mine,' 'Heart of My Heart'…

"Those songs are all so sad now. Even fifty years ago those songs were sad."

She is composed, and ready to greet people as the film ends and the lights come up.

"Madge, honey, I thought we'd never see each other again. Are you sneaking away to speakeasies in Chicago when we have a few days off?"

Madge laughs, and then rises to hug Allan Dwan, who directed her in *Summer Bachelors* (1926).

She starts to cry, as they exchange hugs. "Oh, Allan, I behaved so very badly in those days."

Allan Dwan is embarrassed. "Madge, it's a long time ago. We're both past it."

"Will you ever forgive me?" she asks.

"Of course, I forgive you. Didn't I come over to say hello?"

Watching Allan Dwan return to where he had been sitting, Madge turns to my wife and says, "I threw it all away. I never took my work seriously. I always went for the good times and the fun. And I've lived long enough to see everything pass me by, and not have very much to show for it. I was my own worst enemy.

"But I have a chance to write my memoirs. The only problem is I don't have many of my films to easily look at. Do you have any of my films? I can always locate *The Iron Horse* and *Lorna Doone*, but I've seen them to death.

"People are going to want more than that, but I can't remember anything. Honestly, I don't know what I did."

Someone is approaching her with a photograph of her as Lorna Doone. She signs the photograph, and returns it.

"Here's my address in Ontario. It's in California. Would either of you write to me, and tell me what I did? It'll bring everything back, the way it was.

"Writing your autobiography is like having a second chance…"

■

Index

Printed in the United States
56098LVS00003B/108

9 781593 930134